Red Men

and

Hat-Wearers

Viewpoints in Indian History

Papers from the Colorado State University Conference on Indian History, August 1974

Edited by Daniel Tyler

© 1976 by Daniel Tyler

First Edition

1 2 3 4 5 6 7 8 9

Printed in the U.S.A.

Line drawings by Dale Crawford
Cover Design by Robert Coonts

Library of Congress Cataloging in Publication Data

Main entry under title:

Red men and hat-wearers.

    Bibliography: p.
    Includes index.
    1. Indians of North America — Historiography — Congresses. I.
Tyler, Daniel. II. Colorado State University, Fort Collins.
E77.R42   970'.004'97   76-10253
ISBN 0-87108-501-1

Drawing on page 148 courtesy of *Wassaja*.

Contents

Part II: The Indian Response

Introduction

Daniel Tyler, Colorado State University

In the summer of 1972, Colorado State University hosted its first conference on western history. As part of a university-wide emphasis on the American West, this conference provided a forum for the discussion of historical trends, research facilities, and archival materials available to students and scholars. One of the sessions was dedicated to the teaching and writing of Indian history. Clyde D. Dollar, then historian at the University of South Dakota (now a Ph.D. candidate at the University of Arkansas), presented a paper entitled "Through the Looking-Glass: History and the Modern Brule Sioux."[1]

Dollar articulated a thesis which proved to be quite controversial. Like Alice of Wonderland fame, he said, the non-Indian historian of today must pass through a cultural mirror in order to fully understand the thinking of the American Indian. There the historian will find that ". . . the concept of history has a decidedly different shape and function. . . ." Furthermore, Dollar added:

> The long association with story-telling and myth-making has caused history to be thought of principally as a means of entertainment, or a method of keeping alive those cultural traditions collectively thought worthy of being perpetuated. Integral to this concept is the idea of an historical fact, which, from the Indian side of the looking glass, is something one has been told by his elders and therefore is not to be questioned. Indeed, among the High Plains people, there is little interest in the subject matter of history per se beyond the repeating of its stories, and a deeply searching pursuit of data and facts on which to build veracity in history is frequently considered rather pointless, perhaps ludicrous, decidedly nosy, and an occupation closely associated with eccentric white men.[2]

1

Dollar's thesis that history from the Indian point of view is more the telling of stories and making of myths than the search for veracity regarding the past stimulated a very lively debate among conference participants. Reverberations continue today. But the excitement over Dollar's ideas served a useful purpose in the sense that they provided an excellent theme for a second summer conference on western history. Thus it was that Colorado State University hosted the "Viewpoints in Indian History" Conference in 1974, and with the generous assistance of the Colorado Humanities Program, invited Indians and non-Indians to address themselves to the question that Dollar had raised two years earlier: "Are Indians and Whites indeed polarized over the meaning and function of history?"

This book is offered to students, teachers, and laymen as a partial record of the conference proceedings. It does not purport to include all the discussion which took place, but Colorado State University does have a complete record of all the proceedings on tape. Interested persons can contact the Office of Educational Media for a catalogue of sessions, speakers, and the prices of individual tapes.

What is represented herein is the editor's view of that portion of the discussion which relates to the concept of cultural Weltanschaung (world view) and how, in particular, the Indian perception of the world affects their writing of history. Readers of this volume should be aware that they are essentially reviewing the highlights of a conference held over a period of two and one-half days. The editor has selected those contributions which seemed most appropriate to the theme, but this in no way implies that what was left out of the book is of lesser quality. Since the objective of this publication is to encourage a greater degree of sensitivity on the part of both Indian and non-Indian historians, conference discussions of art, film-making, women's rights, educational legislation, etc., have been introduced on a very limited basis and in summary form.

In addition to this introduction, the reader will find two distinct sections in the pages that follow. The first incorporates the six formal papers by non-Indian scholars who were invited to speak on either White or Indian viewpoints toward cultural contact during a specific historical period. John C. Ewers presents the first paper, "Indian Views of the White Man Prior to 1850: An Interpretation." This is followed by David Miller's "The Fur Men and Explorers View the Indians," which treats approximately the same time period. Donald J. Berthrong then presents "Changing Concepts: The Indians Learn About the 'Long Knives' and Settlers (1849-1890s)," which is followed by Robert L. Munkres' "The Arrival of Emigrants and Soldiers: Curiosity, Contempt, Confusion, and Conflict." The final grouping pairs Joseph H. Cash's "The Reservation Indian Meets the White Man," and W. David Baird's "The Quest for a Red-Faced White Man: Reservation Whites View Their Indian Wards."

It is important for the reader to bear in mind that Indian authors were purposely excluded from this section. Ewers, Miller, Berthrong, Munkres, Cash, and Baird were expected to use traditional types of documentary source material, and they were expected to pursue historical veracity in the best tradition of western world historians. Although this volume actually devotes more space to their point of view, the conference itself gave more time to the Indian speakers, who not only critiqued the formal papers, but also discussed in some detail the Indian view on a number of related subjects. Thus the reader should weigh the historical techniques of these traditional historians against the logic and world view of Indian commentators.

It is in the second section, therefore, that the Indian viewpoints will be encountered. Beginning with what this editor considers to be the most salient features of their commentary (and there are admitted risks in assuming that a non-Indian can accomplish this), the second section also includes Vine Deloria Jr.'s banquet address challenge to historians to get into "the twentieth century" and R. David Edmunds' excellent analysis of "Indian Humor: Can the Red Man Laugh?" — an entertaining and somewhat controversial piece in itself.

Unfortunately, there are thousands and thousands of persons whose views are not represented herein. However, it is hoped that this volume can be used to stimulate further discussion of the importance of world view in historical writing. Although the regional emphasis in these papers is on the Indian cultures of the High Plains and the White intrusion thereon, the main ideas seem to be appropriate to most areas where Indian and non-Indian contact occurred for a prolonged period of time.

Preparation for and execution of the conference was a major task which could not have taken place without the assistance of my friend and fellow historian Clyde D. Dollar. Nor could we have succeeded without the interest of Pat Shanks and

Anne Lewis, both of the Colorado Humanities Program. We are also indebted to the Colorado State University Office of Conferences and Institutes — most particularly, Caroline Frye, whose charm and efficiency never faded, even under the most exasperating circumstances. I am personally indebted to Christina Case, my associate director, who arranged most of the details during my absence in Mexico and on whom fell the major responsibility of running the actual show. Without these people, the conference would have been a failure, and this volume would not have seen the light of day.

Daniel Tyler
Fort Collins, Colorado

---

[1] Published in Daniel Tyler, ed., *Western History in the Seventies* (Fort Collins, Colo.: Educational Media and Information Systems, 1973), pp. 38-45.

[2] *Ibid.*, pp. 39-40.

Part One

Non-Indian Viewpoints
Of
Indian-White Contact

Indian Views of the White Man Prior to 1850: An Interpretation

John C. Ewers, Smithsonian Institution

I am calling this paper "an interpretation," because I recognize the difficulties of trying to walk in the moccasins and to think the thoughts of people who lived more than one and one-quarter centuries ago. I have been studying the Indians of the Northern Plains for more than 40 years, but I have never talked to an Indian who was old enough to recall what *he* was thinking and other members of his tribe were saying before 1850. How then am I to know what Assiniboine, Cree and Dakota Indians who met Frenchmen before 1700, Mandans who saw French traders in their villages in 1738, or even Crows who observed the first white explorers in their country in 1805, thought of those palefaces?

Paradoxical as it may seem, any interpretation of Indian views of Whites prior to 1850 *must* rely heavily upon the writings of some of the people who were the *objects* of the Indian's appraisals — white men. I believe, however, that a number of white writers reported objectively and with candor the views expressed by the Indians they met, and that some of those views are confirmed by evidence from Indian languages, and by the Indians' own literature — picture writing. I believe also that Indian attitudes were reflected in their actions and that we do have a rich record of Indian behavior toward Whites on the Northern Great Plains before 1850.

It will simplify my problem some if I may confine my remarks to those tribes whose histories and cultures I have studied most intensively. These are the tribes who, in 1850, lived in the region my teacher, Clark Wissler, used to refer to as the Missouri-Saskatchewan area, which includes the valleys of the Saskatchewan River and its tributaries in present Canada and the valleys of the Upper Missouri and its tributaries in the United States. Many of the best-known tribes of the American West lived in that region. They included the Arikara, Hidatsa, and Mandan, who were sedentary farmers; and the nomadic, buffalo-hunting Plains Cree, Plains Ojibwa, Assiniboine, the three Blackfoot tribes, Gros Ventres (Atsina), Crow, and Teton Dakota (or Western Sioux).

Throughout the historic period prior to 1850, the tribes of this region prided themselves upon their independence, their skill as hunters, their astuteness as traders, and their prowess as warriors. Archeological evidence of strongly fortified prehistoric villages on the Missouri in the Dakotas indicates that intertribal warfare existed in this region centuries before the arrival of Whites. It continued for more than three decades after 1850. For thousands of years, Indians hunted buffalo in this region, and this animal was still the staff of life for the nomadic tribes of this area in 1850. None of those tribes had ceded their hunting grounds to the Whites in 1850. It was not until 1851 that the boundaries of many of those tribes were first defined by treaty, and the Blackfoot tribes did not negotiate their first treaty with the United States until 1855.

Present-day Indians, convinced of the need for pan-Indian organizations to protect Indian rights and to seek solutions to pressing Indian problems, may find it hard to conceive of a time when "Indianness" was not of prime importance to Indians. There was no basis, however, for such an ethnocentric concept *before* the Whites arrived. Then all the Indians' friends and enemies were other Indians. Rather, Indians were then "tribocentric," if I may coin a term. They tended to remain so throughout the period of White contact well beyond 1850. The Indian owed his allegiance not to his race but to his family, his band or village, and his tribe. A warrior was proud to be a Crow, a Mandan, a Cree, or a Dakota. Each tribe spoke its own dialect, and regarded its members as "the people." Members of others tribes were outsiders. Whether they were friends or enemies depended upon the extent to which their tribal interests were in harmony or conflict with one's own. Tribes in continual competition for hunting grounds became hereditary enemies — as Cree versus Dakota, or Blackfoot versus Crow. Some tribes became allies of neighboring tribes for their mutual protection

8

against strong, common enemies — such as Cree and Assiniboine, Blackfoot and Gros Ventres, Mandan and Hidatsa. Trading with the enemy was not unknown, however. The Mandan and Dakota negotiated temporary truces in order to exchange garden produce for products of the chase to their mutual advantage.

Inasmuch as the very great majority of Whites known to Indians of this region prior to 1850 were traders, it is well to know that these Indians were experienced traders when they first met white men. Finds of marine shells from both the Pacific and Gulf Coasts in prehistoric village sites on the Missouri indicate that extended trade routes led to and from these villages of farming tribes in pre-White times. Pre-eighteenth-century village sites also have yielded trade materials from less distant sources: obsidian, probably from present Yellowstone National Park in western Wyoming, and red pipestone from the famed catlinite quarry in southwestern Minnesota.[1]

Through intertribal trade northward from the Southwest, the European horse reached the Crow and Blackfoot tribes in the western part of this area *before* those Indians met white men. By the time the first Whites arrived in their country, members of those tribes were riding horses on the buffalo chase and to war and were using horses as burden-bearers in their camp movements. Horses had also become prized booty in warfare.

Through intertribal trade, also, limited quantities of European-made manufactured goods reached the tribes in the central and western portions of this area before they met Whites. These items were brought by Indian intermediaries who traded directly with Whites at distant trading posts. When Pierre La Verendrye accompanied an Assiniboine trading party to the Mandan villages in 1738, he observed that the Mandans were "sharp traders and clean the Assiniboine out of everything they have in the way of guns, powder, ball, knives, axes, and awls."[2]

The villages of the farming tribes were flourishing trading centers before the Whites arrived. By the time the Whites appeared, these and neighboring nomadic tribes had obtained enough articles of European manufacture to be sure of their usefulness as weapons, tools, or utensils, or their attractiveness as luxuries, and to whet their desire for more of these goods.

The Indians were experienced barterers, knew something of values and markups, and were prepared to pay for what they wanted. These Indians had become literally "horse traders" — with all of the keen bargaining sense that term implies.[3]

Another very important aspect of Indian culture in this region at the time of first contact with Whites conditioned Indian reactions to Whites during the early years of interracial relations. I refer to the Indians' world view — their belief in supernatural powers, or medicine in the religious sense. They envisioned the world around them — the sky, the land, and water — as the abode of powers which were stronger than their own, and which could help or harm them. They sought to placate malevolent powers, such as thunder and serpent-like underwater monsters; they sought the aid of benevolent ones, such as sun, birds, and animals. Any object that was unique or strange to them was looked upon as medicine that inspired both awe and reverence. The individual who owned such an object, professed to know its origin and function, and used it to his own advantage was thought to be blessed with supernatural power.

Given this prevailing Indian world view, or body of beliefs, it should not seem strange to us that the Indians of this region looked upon the white men's many technological inventions as awesome medicines; that they sought to obtain strange objects from the white man's culture for their own medicines, or that they regarded white men who appeared to be skillful users of these objects as possessors of very potent supernatural powers.

The literature of Indian-White contacts in this region is rich in white men's observations on these points. Among the many wonders of the white men's world which Indians once looked upon as medicine were the gun, iron pot, compass, telescope, burning glass, magnet, thermometer, sextant, music box, watch, steamboat, white artists' portraits of Indians, and any specimen of handwriting. Whites sometimes took advantage of the Indians' ignorance of some of these wonders which remained incomprehensible to them, even after many years of contact. At the end of our period, Edwin T. Denig, the factor at Fort Union, wrote that Indians in that neighborhood could "be made to believe almost any story, however absurd, if read in appearance from a book."[4]

Ingenious Indians were eager to adopt strange objects from the white man's world as personal war medicines. Francois Larocque, the first white man known to have visited the

Crow Country, observed in 1805 that one Crow warrior had as his medicine a fragment of colored glass from a magic lantern; another wore the tail of a Spanish cow as a hair pendant.[5] Surely neither of these war medicines was more remarkable than was that of a Dakota chief to whom Father De Smet later gave a religious medal. That chief opened a box, unwrapped a buckskin covering, and unrolled a colored picture of General Diebitsch, a prominent Russian leader in the Napoleonic Wars, in full uniform and astride a beautiful horse. He explained to De Smet that for years this had been his war medicine. He offered his pipe to that general "before all his enterprises against his enemies, and attributed to him the many victories he had gained."[6]

Father Hennepin (in 1680) and the French trader Pierre-Charles Le Sueur (in 1700) knew the Dakota in Minnesota. Both claimed the Dakota called them "spirits."[7] James Kipp, regarded as the traders' best authority on the Mandan dialect of Siouan in 1833, translated their term for white man — wasschi — as "he who has everything, or everything good."[8]

Jean Baptiste Truteau, pioneer white trader among the Arikara, wrote of them in 1796: "They have a great respect and a great veneration for all white men in general, whom they put in the rank of divinity, and all that comes from them is regarded by these same people as miraculous. They do not know how to distinguish among civilized nations, English, French, Spanish, et cetera, whom they call indifferently white men or spirits."[9]

The persistence of the term Napikwan (old man person) for the white man among the Blackfoot shows that they likened him to an ambivalent wonder worker in their own mythology. Napi was also a clever trickster with very human frailties. Likewise the Algonquian-speaking Gros Ventres, Arapaho, and Cheyenne named the white man after their trickster, Spider or "the wise one."

So much has been written in recent years about the Indians' contributions to world medicine that we may tend to forget that in this region during the early decades of White contact Indians regarded the white man's remedies for physical ailments as superior to their own. Lewis and Clark were repeatedly beseeched by Indians to treat their sick. Alexander Henry, a trader among the Blackfoot, wrote in 1811: ". . . they are perpetually begging medicine from us, and place the greatest confidence in whatever we give them, imagining that everything medical which comes from the trader must be a sovereign remedy for all diseases."[10] In that same year, John Bradbury, an English botanist, made friends with an Arikara shaman while he was collecting plants near the villages of that tribe. The Indian looked upon Bradbury as a fellow practitioner and proudly revealed the contents of his deerskin medicine bag to him.[11]

Father Nicholas Point, the first Christian missionary among the Blackfoot on the Missouri in 1845-1846, found that these Indians looked upon him much as they did their own medicine men. They thought he could cause disease or make the thunder roll if he became angry. They believed he possessed the power to cure sickness and implored him to treat them. They thought that baptism, like the traditional Indian sweatbath, would insure bodily health.[12] We know, too, that for several decades, beginning at least as early as the early 1830s, the Blackfoot, who were fearful of handling their own dead, brought the bodies of prominent chiefs to Fort Benton where the white traders prepared them for burial.[13]

As Indians became better acquainted with Whites, they became more impressed with their human qualities. Indeed, the Arikara appear to have removed Frenchmen from their pantheon of divinities by the year 1804. Pierre-Antoine Tabeau, who was trading with the Arikara when the Lewis and Clark Expedition reached their villages on their upriver journey that fall, observed: "It is only a little while since the Ricara deified the French, who, unhappily, have only too well disabused them by their conduct and their talk. Thus they have passed today from one extreme to the other and we are indeed nothing in their eyes."[14]

He noted that the only member of the Lewis and Clark party whom the Arikara regarded with great awe was "a large, fine man, black as a bear." He referred to York, Clark's Negro servant, the first black man the Indians of the Upper Missouri tribes had seen.[15] Because Negroes entered their country in the company of Whites, they came to be known as "black white men" to those Indians.

The Mandans, near whom the Lewis and Clark party wintered in 1804-1805, retained a higher regard for the supernatural powers of Whites than did the Arikaras. In their buffalo-calling ceremony, it was the custom for younger married women to have sexual relations with older men of the tribe who were thought to possess very potent supernatural powers, so that the women in turn might transmit these powers to their husbands. They invited men of the Lewis and Clark party to play the roles of some of the older men in this religious ceremony.[16] Other writers on the Mandans around the turn of the century may have maligned their women by alluding to their easy virtue. These women also may have been interested in white men as sources of supernatural power.

As Indians became better acquainted with Whites, they came to believe that some white men had stronger powers than did others. During the winter that the Lewis and Clark party resided near the Mandan and Hidatsa villages, their blacksmiths were kept busy making and repairing metal articles for the Indians in exchange for corn. Indians looked upon the smiths' bellows as medicine. A Hidatsa chief offered his frank opinion of the men of the American expedition to a British trader who was in his village: "There are only two sensible men amongst them, the worker in iron and the mender of guns."[17]

White artists were another occupational group whom Indians thought were gifted with exceptional powers. The Indians of this region had both religious and secular art traditions in which human figures were depicted. Successful warriors portrayed their coups in battle. Some Indians made crude representations of their personal enemies so that they might destroy them through witchcraft. Indian art could serve good or evil ends.

In their own art, as in their gesture language, they distinguished the White from the Indian by representing the former as a hat-wearer. In their sign language, the white man was designated simply by passing the right hand across the brow, palm down, to convey the idea of a hat brim or visor. This was, of course, a purely descriptive gesture. Whether the white man was friend or enemy depended upon the larger context in which the gesture was used. In the winter counts of the Teton Dakota, white men were pictured as hat-wearers. Several winter counts picture the first white trader to establish a post in Dakota territory on the Missouri, and who supplied these Indians with guns. Known to the Dakotas as The Good White Man, he was probably Regis Loisel, a Frenchman from St. Louis, who built that trading post at the beginning of the 19th century.[18]

Indians had traditionally pictured humans with knob-like heads devoid of individual features. When white artists came among them who created life-like portraits in two dimensions, some Indians refused to sit for their portraits, fearing that the reproduction of their likenesses would deprive them of their power. George Catlin wrote of his difficulties in convincing the Mandans that they would not be harmed if he painted their portraits. On the other hand, a Blackfoot warrior, the following summer (1833), bragged that he had survived a battle with the Assiniboine and Cree outside Fort McKenzie without a wound *because* "Mr. Bodmer had taken his portrait." At the Hidatsa villages the next fall, Bodmer painted birds and animals for Indians, which they thought "would make them proof against musket balls." These were probably the birds and animals that were those warriors' guardian spirits.[19]

In the British possessions in 1848, Paul Kane apparently convinced the Cree that by sketching their sacred pipestems he was enhancing their potency as war medicines.[20] Yet Rudolph Kurz encountered violent opposition from the Hidatsa when a cholera epidemic broke out among them as he was beginning to picture those Indians in 1851. They recalled that a disastrous smallpox epidemic had occurred in 1837, after both Catlin and Bodmer had painted members of their tribe, and they threatened to kill Kurz if he continued to draw them. The Swiss artist was forced to move up river to Fort Union; he encountered no such resistance on the part of the Assiniboine, Cree, and Crow Indians who traded there.[21]

Whether Indians looked upon white artists' works as good or bad medicine appears to have depended upon the circumstances under which they were made. In any case, a common interest in art seems to have afforded a basis for close rapport between some Indian and white artists, and the more detailed and more realistic renderings of humans and horses that began to appear in the works of Indian artists *after* they had opportunities to observe closely how the white artists worked, and after they gained access to smooth paper and precise drawing instruments (pencils and crayons), must have been in part due to white influence.[22]

It appears clear to me from an examination of the written record that white traders' penetration deeper and deeper into this region, in order to profit from direct trade with more and more tribes, threatened the interests of many tribes and roused both ill feelings and open hostilities toward the Whites. Different tribes were affected in different ways and at different times as this movement progressed. This movement first threatened and then eliminated the profitable activities of the peripheral tribes in supplying manufacturered goods to the more remote ones. It also upset the delicate balance of powers that had existed in the intertribal warfare of this region. Furthermore, the actions of these tribes indicate that they were fully aware of these threats to their interests.

In this region, the fur trade initially expanded from east to west. Those tribes on the eastern periphery of the region were the first to receive guns and other metal weapons. They were strengthened at the expense of their more remote Indian enemies who lacked those weapons. Surely the Assiniboine saw the advantage of gaining access to the flow of firearms from Hudson Bay when, even before 1700, they abandoned their Dakota allies and allied themselves with their former Cree enemies. By the early years of the 18th century, the Cree and Assiniboine also were receiving improved war materials from French traders operating from Montreal. As early as 1736, a Dakota war party wiped out a party of Frenchmen and mutilated their bodies. One of those Frenchmen was a son of La Verendrye. Two years earlier he had joined a Cree campaign against the Dakota. The message of that Dakota action was clear — Whites must not take sides in Indian warfare.[23]

There were early indications that the peripheral tribes were aware of the potential loss of profits to them if Whites extended their trade to the more remote tribes. In 1797, the Assiniboine traders tried to dissuade David Thompson from visiting the important Mandan trading center by telling him of the danger of meeting Dakota war parties en route. In 1805, Mandan and Hidatsa traders, in turn, sought to prevent Larocque from going on to the Crow Country by representing the Crows as thieves and liars and stressing the dangers of encountering hostile tribes. We know that the extension of the white man's trade did eliminate Assiniboine intermediaries from the trade with both the Mandans and the Blackfoot tribes, and the importance of the old Mandan trading center declined rapidly after Whites opened direct trade with the still more remote tribes who had traded there.

Those tribes who had established direct trade with Whites resented white traders' efforts to penetrate deeper into the

Indian country to supply their enemies with war-making materials. Doubtless those Teton Dakota who sought to prevent the passage of Lewis and Clark's boats up the Missouri in 1804 looked upon those Whites as traders who would supply their Mandan and Hidatsa enemies. The Blackfoot tribes tried to prevent British traders from carrying arms and ammunition to enemy tribes west of the Rockies, although the traders circumvented the Blackfoot blockade by crossing the mountains farther north and outside Blackfoot territory.[24]

I have quoted Tabeau's observation that the Arikara were disenchanted with the Whites as early as 1804. By that time, his firm was already doing business with their enemies, the Teton, farther up the Missouri. Another factor helped to rouse the Arikara to open hostility. An Arikara chief died during a trip to Washington in 1805, and the Arikara thought the Whites had killed him.

Arikara hostility toward Whites continued until the smallpox epidemic of 1837 greatly reduced the population of that tribe. When Lieutenant Pryor tried to return the Mandan chief, Shahaka, who had been to Washington, to his people in 1807, the angry Arikara opened fire on his party and forced them to turn back to St. Louis. In 1823, Ashley's large party of trappers who were bound up river were stopped by the Arikara at their villages; in the ensuing battle, thirteen or fourteen of those Whites were killed or mortally wounded. This action precipitated the only U.S. Army campaign against a tribe of this region prior to 1850. Col. Henry Leavenworth's soldiers, augmented by mountain men and a large contingent of Dakota Indian allies, moved against the Arikara villages. The Dakota warriors were eager to attack, but Leavenworth delayed, and the Arikara slipped away in the middle of the night. A lasting result of this inaction was the contempt for the courage of white soldiers that persisted in the minds of aggressive Dakota warriors. Arikara-Dakota warfare continued for three generations. By the 1860s, Arikara chiefs were pleading for white soldiers to help defend their people against repeated Dakota attacks.[25]

The Blackfoot tribes and their Gros Ventres allies, who hunted on both sides of the international boundary, had traded with the British in the Saskatchewan Valley for a half-century before American mountain men roused their hostility — and with good reason. The Americans were supplying war materials to their Crow, Shoshoni, and Flathead enemies. The Blackfoot also profited by robbing the mountain men and taking their beaver pelts and other booty to friendly Whites in the north to exchange for arms, ammunition, and other desirable goods. During the quarter-century prior to 1831, numerous skirmishes took place between the Blackfoot (and/or Gros Ventres) and the trappers near the Missouri headwaters and in the mountains. Twice during that period (in 1811 and 1823) the Indians chased the trappers out of present-day Montana, leaving numbers of dead Whites in the field. Not until 1831 were Americans able to open peaceful trade with the Blackfoot tribes. By then it was clear that a major cause of Blackfoot resentment had been the trappers' exploitation of the rich fur resources of their hunting grounds from which the Indians derived no share of the profits. As a Blackfoot chief confided to Indian Agent Sanford in 1834, "If you will send Traders into our Country we will protect them and treat them well; but for Trappers — Never."[26]

Much has been written about the profits Whites made from the fur trade. It would be difficult to believe that Indians did not profit from that trade, also, before 1850. They offered furs, buffalo hides, and pemmican from animals which were abundant in their country in exchange for manufactured goods which they wanted. Standards of value were established by agreement between Indians and Whites. The records of the trading companies contain many references to Indian refusals to accept articles they did not want, or ones of inferior quality. Firearms experts rate the popular Northwest trade gun as an efficient as well as a cheap weapon. The Crows and the Mandans (in the early 1830s) refused to accept liquor in their trade. Competition among white traders gave Indians a choice of markets, and it checked inflation of prices on manufactured goods. Indians employed metal tools and ornaments, cloth, twine, thread, beads, and other materials as replacements for aboriginal materials in ways that saved them labor and enriched their lives. At the same time, they became more and more dependent upon Whites for both luxuries and necessities other than food.[27]

The conduct of the trade brought some Indians into much closer relationships with Whites than it did others. In the beginning, white traders visited Indian villages where they were protected and their actions regulated by members of the tribal Soldier Societies. After white traders built posts surrounded with palisades to protect them from attacks by hostile Indians, prominent Indian warriors continued to play important roles in regulating trade. I refer especially to the "Soldiers of the Fort," Indians who were recognized as tribal leaders, but who also served the interests of the Whites. Not only did they encourage members of their tribes to trade at particular posts, but they kept their white employers informed of tribal wants and activities, and they served as policemen who kept order and prevented thefts of white men's property while other Indians were at the forts.

Two of the best-known Indians of this region in the 1830s were "Soldiers of the Fort" for the American Fur Company. One was Four Bears, second chief of the Mandans, who claimed the best war record of any man in his tribe, and who served as a director of his people's major annual religious ceremony, the Okipa. Another was The Light; he was the son of the prominent Assiniboine chief who selected the site for Fort Union, the principal trading post on the Upper Missouri for several decades after 1827. Both of these men were tragic figures. Four Bears died in the smallpox epidemic of 1837 that decimated his tribe. Shortly before his death, he cursed the Whites as black-hearted dogs for repaying his long and faithful friendship with this fatal pestilence. The Light was the first member of his tribe to visit Washington and the cities of the East, in 1831-1832. After his return, he was killed by a man of his own tribe who refused to believe his oft-repeated stories of the wonders of the white man's world.[28]

Many Indian women had even more intimate relations with Whites that were longer lasting and ended more happily. I refer to the hundreds of Indian women of all of the tribes of this area who married white men. There is no complete record of the total number of these interracial marriages before 1850. Some of the brides were members of chiefly families whose marriages to prominent traders enhanced the positions of their relatives. Most of these Indian women married Whites who held less important positions in the fur trade, clerks or laborers. White men were considered good catches because it was thought that their wives would not have to work so hard and that they would be better fed and dressed than were the wives of Indians.

Some of these interracial marriages did not last; others proved to be partnerships for life. In either case, we know that they were productive; there was a growing number of individuals of mixed Indian and White descent in the population of this region. Sons of Indian women and white traders themselves became employees in the fur trade as factors, clerks, guides, interpreters, hunters, and laborers. Well before 1850, large communities of Métis or Red River half-breeds were formed in the eastern portion of this region. They developed a way of life that was marginal to both Indian and white cultural traditions. They lived in log cabins, grew some crops, and took part in prolonged, semiannual buffalo hunting excursions, during which they killed large numbers of buffalo and carried tons of meat and hides homeward in their creaking, two-wheeled carts. Still other sons and daughters of mixed marriages became leaders in their mothers' tribes in later generations.[29]

It seems clear to me from my examination of the written record that Indian attitudes toward Whites changed over the years prior to 1850. If indeed Indians of this region tended to view Whites as divinities or supermen during the earliest years of contact between the races, Indians became increasingly aware of the white men's human qualities as they became better acquainted. It is also clear that different tribes and different individuals within those tribes held different opinions of Whites. The Cree warrior who benefitted from the white man's war materials during the early years must have held a more favorable view of Whites than did the Dakota brave who believed the Whites were helping his Indian enemies. The Blackfoot warrior of the 1820s certainly distinguished between the Hudson's Bay Company trader and the American trapper who exploited his hunting grounds without any advantage to him. The chief who was acknowledged by the trader with gifts of a medal, a handsome suit of clothes, and kegs of liquor, must have had a more friendly feeling toward that White than did his younger rival for band or tribal leadership who had received no favors from the trader. The Indian woman married to a white man certainly understood white men's customs and values better than did her tribal age-mate whose husband was an Indian. Indian attitudes toward Whites probably varied as greatly as did white men's attitudes toward Indians prior to 1850.

This is not to say that misconceptions about Indians did not persist in the minds of white traders who lived in the Indian Country. Even so, those traders had better opportunities to gain an understanding of Indians than Indian traders had of understanding either that larger culture of which the White trader was a part or the many Whites outside the Indian Country who also had interests in the fur trade. The White trader in the Indian Country could visit every camp or village of a tribe — to estimate their numbers, to reckon their potential for trade or war. He knew their leaders, and he observed their customs at first hand. The Indian trader, on the other hand, met in the white trader only that tip of the white man's far-flung and complex civilization that protruded into the Indian Country. He never met the English gunsmith, the Venetian beadmaker, the New England textile weaver, the Brazilian tobacco grower, the New Jersey maker of shell hairpipes, the Missouri lead miner, or the London, New York, or St. Louis investor — all of whom had stakes in the Indian trade. Before 1850, few Indians of this region had ever seen a white woman. Nor could the stay-at-home Indians of this region believe the seemingly fantastic stories told by the few Indians who had visited St. Louis, Philadelphia, New York, and Washington of the white men's teeming cities, his many-storied houses, his vast industrial and war potential.

A few Indians of this region learned of the white men's concepts of the universe, which differed markedly from their own, and these Indians reacted differently. At Fort Clark during the winter of 1833-1834, the German scientist, Prince Maximilian of Wied-Neuwied, and his artist-companion, Karl Bodmer, exchanged ideas about the heavenly bodies and the origin of the universe with friendly Mandan Indians. The Prince reported: "They laughed outright when we affirmed that the earth was round and revolved about the sun. Others, however, would not reject our views, and were of the opinion that, as Whites could do so much that was incomprehensible to them, it was possible they might be right on this point also."[30]

By the mid-nineteenth century, most of the tribes of this region had known Whites for more than a century. They knew that Whites differed from Indians culturally as well as physically, and that cultural differences went well beyond the fact that Whites were hat-wearers. In their conceptions of these differences, they revealed something of their attitudes toward Whites. In 1854, a statement of an Indian viewpoint of these differences was written by Edwin T. Denig, who was probably the most knowledgeable white student of the tribes of the Upper Missouri at that time. The son of a Pennsylvania physician, he had traded with the tribes on the Missouri for more than two decades. He had married two Assiniboine women, and he fathered four children by them. Denig presented the Indian viewpoint in these words:

> Now this Supernatural Unknown Cause or Mystery created all things in the beginning. After the earth a few men and women of different colors were made, from whom descended all people. Different races were created for different purposes. They say that the whites were allotted education, knowledge of the mechanical arts, of machinery, etc., and therefore the whites are in many ways Wah-con. They were also made rich and clothed, or have the means of getting clothing, and everything they want without hardship or exposure. The Indians, they say, were made naked and with such qualifications as to suit a hunter, knowledge enough to make his arms and use them at war or in the chase, a constitution to stand severe cold, long fasting, excessive fatigue, and watchfulness, and this was his portion. The position and pursuits of people were not defined by any laws, oral or otherwise delivered, but each with the powers granted to him was enabled to live.[31]

Notes

[1] W. Raymond Wood, "Northern Plains Village Cultures Internal Stability and External Relationships," *Journal of Anthropological Research* (University of New Mexico. Albuquerque), vol. 30, no. 1 (Spring, 1974): 1-16.

[2] L. J. Burpee, ed., *Journals and Letters of Pierre Gaultier de Varennes de la Verendrye and his Sons* (Toronto, 1927), p. 332.

[3] John C. Ewers, "The Influence of the Fur Trade upon the Indians of the Northern Plains," in *People and Pelts*. Selected Papers from the North American Fur Trade Conference. Malvina Bolus, ed. (Winnipeg, 1972).

[4] Edwin T. Denig, *Indian Tribes of the Upper Missouri*. 48th Annual Report, Bureau of American Ethnology (Washington, D.C., 1930), p. 528. John C. Ewers, "When Red and White Men Met," *The Western Historical Quarterly* 2, no. 2 (April 1971), pp. 136-138.

[5] Francois Larocque, *Journal of Larocque from the Assiniboine to the Yellowstone*. Publication No. 3. Canadian Archives (Ottawa, 1910), pp. 62-66.

[6] Pierre Jean De Smet, *Western Missions and Missionaries*. (New York, 1862), p. 46.

[7] Louis Hennepin, *A New Discovery of the Vast Country in America,* ed. Reuben Gold Thwaites, 2 vols. (Chicago, 1903), vol. 1, p. 292. Mildred Mott Wedel, "Le Sueur and the Dakota Sioux," in *Aspects of Upper Great Lakes Anthropology*. Papers in Honor of Lloyd A. Wilford. Minnesota Historical Society. (St. Paul, 1974), p. 171.

[8] Maximilian, Prince of Wied-Neuwied, "Travels in the Interior of North America," in *Early Western Travels,* ed. Reuben Gold Thwaites, vols. 22-24 (Cleveland, 1906), 24:246.

[9] A. P. Nasatir, ed., *Before Lewis and Clark.* Documents Illustrating the History of the Missouri, 1785-1804, 2 vols. (St. Louis, 1952), 2:382.

[10] Alexander Henry and David Thompson, *New Light on the Early History of the Greater Northwest,* ed. Elliott Coues, 3 vols. (New York, 1897), 2:731.

[11] John Bradbury, "Travels in the Interior of America, in the years 1809, 1810, and 1811," in *Early Western Travels,* ed. Reuben Gold Thwaites, vol. 5, pp. 132-133.

[12] Pierre Jean DeSmet, *Life, Letters, and Travels of Father Pierre Jean De Smet,* ed. H. M. Chittenden and A. T. Richardson, 4 vols. (New York, 1905), 3:953-954.

[13] Maximilian, Prince of Wied-Neuwied, *Travels,* vol. 23, pp. 140-142. Testimony to author of *Richard Sanderville,* Piegan (1940s).

[14] Annie Heloise Abel, ed., *Tabeau's Narrative of Loisel's Expedition to the Upper Missouri* (Norman, Okla., 1939), pp. 200-201.

[15] *Ibid.,* p. 201.

[16] *Ibid.,* pp. 196-197. In 1833, Prince Maximilian was invited by an Hidatsa woman to assume the role of ceremonial father in that tribe's buffalo calling ceremony. See Maximilian, *Travels,* 24:30.

[17] Charles Mackenzie, "The Missouri Indians, 1804-1805," in Louis R. Masson, *Les bourgeois de la Compagnie du Nord-Ouest,* 2 vols. (Quebec, 1889-1890), 1:330.

[18] John C. Ewers, *Images of the White Man in 19th Century Plains Indian Art* (The Hague, Netherlands: Mouton Publishers (in press). Garrick Mallery, *Picture-Writing of the American Indians.* 10th Annual Report, Bureau of American Ethnology. (Washington, D.C., 1893), pp. 313, 653.

[19] George Catlin in *New York Commercial Advertiser,* Nov. 23, 1832. Maximilian, *Travels,* 23:152, 319; 24:35.

[20] J. Russell Harper, ed, *Paul Kane's Frontier* (Austin, Texas, 1971), p. 144.

[21] Rudolph Friederich Kurz, *Journal of Rudolph Friederich Kurz ... 1846-1852, trans.,* Myrtis Jarrell, ed. J.N.B. Hewitt. Bureau of American Ethnology Bulletin 115 (Washington, D.C., 1937), pp. 76-77, 98, 215.

[22] John C. Ewers, "Plains Indian Painting. The History and Development of an American Art Form." *The American West* 5, no. 2 (March 1968): 4-10.

[23] L. J. Burpee, ed., *Journals and Letters of Pierre Gaultier de*

Varennes de la Verendrye and his Sons, pp. 262-264.

[24] Ewers, *The Influence of the Fur Trade*, p. 4.

[25] Edwin T. Denig, "Of the Arikaras," in *Five Indian Tribes of the Upper Missouri*, ed. John C. Ewers (Norman, Okla., 1961).

[26] John C. Ewers, *The Blackfeet, Raiders on the Northwestern Plains* (Norman, Okla., 1958), pp. 45-57.

[27] John C. Ewers, *The Influence of the Fur Trade*, pp. 7-11.

[28] For further biographical information on Four Bears and The Light see John C. Ewers, *Indian Life on the Upper Missouri* (Norman, Okla., 1968), pp. 75-90, 103-109.

[29] *Ibid.*, pp. 57-67.

[30] Maximilian, *Travels*, 23:288.

[31] Edwin T. Denig, *Indian Tribes of the Upper Missouri*, pp. 486-487.

Dale Crawford 75

The Fur Men and Explorers Meet the Indians

David Miller, Cameron College

Introduction

White men who visited or lived in the trans-Mississippi West during the first half of the nineteenth century were drawn to this region for a variety of reasons. The West offered traders and trappers economic opportunity as well as a chance to lead less restrained lives. For natural scientists and anthropologists, the West provided an immense natural workshop, abounding with new and unusual flora and fauna, and it provided opportunity for fascinating scientific investigation. Writers found grist for exotic and sensational books which were eagerly read in both the United States and Europe. The West also held immense attraction to romantics, who found an outlet for sentimental longings to experience pristine nature far from what they considered as the "debasing" effects of society and civilization, among Indians whom they viewed as natural men, as children of nature.

The extent of their experience or knowledge about American Indians varied considerably. Some travelers acquired only superficial knowledge, while others had opportunity to become intimately acquainted with one or more tribes. Some were better educated and more articulate and sophisticated in their observations, but many had a relatively limited understanding or appreciation of Indian culture. All arrived in Indian Country with biases and presuppositions. Most, nursing their prejudices and preconceptions, found exactly what they had expected to find and reported accordingly. If a man came west expecting to encounter savages and barbarians, he usually found them. If he was looking for examples of natural men, they were everywhere to be seen. Travelers' and fur men's observations about American Indians were frequently colored with trite stereotypes and abusive nineteenth-century rhetoric.

People who gravitated to the frontier and later wrote of their experiences came from different backgrounds and were motivated for different reasons. Each reacted to a specific set of circumstances. Yet all looked for sensation, and all wrote about those things which seemed most unusual, most shocking or most exotic. Most of their statements, descriptions, or observations were therefore tainted with inaccuracies, if only from the point of omission or emphasis.

In preparing this paper, I have concentrated on the accounts of about a dozen men who traveled or lived on the High Plains during the first half of the nineteenth century. Included are trappers and traders, scientists, writers, and romantic artists. Several were foreign born. Although the selection of sources is always subjective, their comments and observations nevertheless reflect a broad spectrum of nineteenth-century opinion. All adhered to the cult of Anglo-Saxon or Teutonic racial superiority. Although many held favorable opinions concerning some facets of Indian culture, the picture they presented was generally not very flattering. They extolled few of the virtues of Indian life, while disparaging most of the vices.

The theme of the Indian as a "noble savage," a child of nature, a natural man, is a theme that appears often in early nineteenth-century travel literature. This concept was a reflection of the European romantic's fascination with nature, as well as his weariness with western European civilization — a feeling which Germans termed "Europamüdigkeit." In questioning the values of civilization, it was quite natural that romantics, in longing to escape what they considered the decadent and debasing effects of western civilization, were drawn to the American frontier. They viewed the free nomadic life of Plains Indians as an ideal; they saw the rejection of civilization's fetters as a life style in harmony with God's creation. The West beyond the Mississippi offered what William H. Goetzmann has termed the "Romantic Horizon."[1] Here a man could experience fresh sensations, exhilarating landscapes, exotic animals, and, of course, find Indians living in a state of nature.

Swiss artist Rudolph Friederich Kurz best expressed this longing:

From my earliest youth primeval forest and Indians had an indescribable charm for me. In spare hours I read only those books that included descriptions and adventures of the new world. . . . Now primeval forests exist only in inaccessible mountain fastnesses; cultivation extends even to the snow-capped peaks. Man's habitations spread over the whole earth; there are churches and schoolhouses without number; yet where are men found dwelling together in unity? Where does sober living pervail? Or contentment? I longed for unknown lands, where no demands of citizenship would involve me in the vortex of political agitations. I longed for the quietude of immemorial woods where no paupers mar one's delight in beauty, where neither climate, false modesty, nor fashion compels concealment of the noblest form of God's creation.[2]

The foremost American expositor of the noble savage was artist George Catlin, who devoted his life to painting Indians of the West and describing their noble character. Catlin defined a "savage" as a "wild man . . . endowed by his Maker with all the humane and noble traits that inhabit the heart of the tame man."[3]

Romantic artist Rudolph Friederich Kurz, although an outspoken critic of Catlin's art, also found nobility traits among western Indians. Kurz visited the Upper Missouri in the mid-1850s in search of the most perfect type of primitive man to portray on his canvas. To Kurz, Indians of the Missouri most closely approximated his ideal, an ideal which he hoped would enable him to create neoclassical art forms. "It was not merely a question as to which zone afforded the most luxuriant landscape and the greatest variety of wild animals," Kurz observed in his journal, "but above all else which country afforded also, the most perfect type of primitive man; for, as my studies progressed, my ideals became more exacting, my aims more lofty: I aspired to attain to the excellence of antique art. . . ." Unlike Catlin, Kurz admitted: "It was no longer my purpose to portray the Indian as an end in itself but to employ that type as a living model in the portrayal of the antique. . . . To depict with my brush the romantic life of the American Indian seemed to me a subject worthy of the manifold studies I was to undertake."[4] For the romantic, to study the noble savage was to rediscover antiquity.

Travelers occasionally expressed what they perceived as similarities between classical antiquity and Indian life styles. In 1811, Henry Brackenridge compared an Arikara village to a Greek city state. "We here see an independent nation, with all the interests and anxieties of the largest," he observed. "How little would its history differ from that of one of Grecian states!"[5] Kurz found the effect of an Indian's blanket similar to a Roman toga, but more graceful, and saw in the Indian woman the classical ideal. Speaking of a trader's wife, he observed: "She would be an excellent model of a Venus, ideal woman of a primitive race; a perfect 'little wife.'" "Ancient Greeks, like the Indians," he continued, "required of the female sex only household virtues, no social qualities; the gentle sex, therefore, exercised no refining influence upon the strong."[6]

Kurz further argued that Indian blood was purer than that of white Americans, reasoning that Indians as the true natives of the soil had a deeper love for their nation, and a greater attachment for their homeland than had the polyglot of American immigrants.[7]

Physically Kurz believed Indians to demonstrate "all that is finest in the human form." Writing of the Iowa tribe, he said their custom of wearing little or no clothing "contributed much toward the proud, easy bearing, as well as to the natural, graceful movements that characterize the Indians."[8] Although Catlin disagreed with Kurz concerning the extent of Indian nudity, he did agree that the "cloth of civilization" veiled and obliterated the grace and beauty of nature and natural men. Therefore, the Indian was "the most beautiful model for the painter," and his homeland was a place of beauty and repose.[9]

Kurz, who relished Indian life along the Missouri, elaborated:

> Here one lives much more at ease, is more free than in the civilized states; the so-called savage is not always disputing about the teachings of religion, about political matters, the rights of man, etc., principles concerning which men should have reached some uniform understanding long ago. With the savage, the sound sense with which Nature endowed him has settled all such matters. Cursing, quarreling, such as one hears constantly among us, is never heard among the Indians.[10]

The Swiss artist was not only critical of what he considered the banalities of civilization, but he believed that civilization stifled a person's ability of natural expression. The Indian, Kurz noted, "because he thinks that waging a constant conflict with his nature is repugnant to common sense," is a "natural man" and much more at inner peace with himself.[11] He lived in a land with pure atmosphere which produced "good health and a long life," where "peace and happiness" reigned supreme. He was independent, unburdened by materialism, high-minded, and a "knight and lord" over his wives and his domain.[12] Above all, Indians were beautiful people. Speaking of the Hidatsa, Kurz noted that they are "magnificent people. . . . These Indians have a noble mien that is classic — all about me are living models of the antique. . . . Their attitudes and movements are never awkward . . . How often I have wished I was a sculptor that I might memorialize in stone the stately pose of certain figures and the masterful fall of the blanket."[13]

Few traders, fur men, or travelers shared the artists' and romantic writers' enthusiasm for Indian nobility. Frequently they criticized Indians for having savage or barbaric attributes, or they ascribed to them certain animal-like qualities. While it can be reasonably assumed that the noble savage never existed as a real person, the same is equally true of his antithesis. Hudson's Bay trader Peter Skene Ogden, who had experienced bitter and deadly encounters with the Blackfeet, depicted them as "beasts of prey."[14] German scientist Maximilian of Wied alluded to the Blackfeet's "perfidious . . . and predatory character," although he conceded that fur trappers were "often greater savages than the Indians themselves."[15] French trader Pierre-Antoine Tabeau was an outspoken critic of the noble savage concept:

> If the Ricara, if the Sioux, is the man of nature so much praised by poets, every poetic license has been taken in painting him; for their picture makes a beautiful contrast to that which I have before me. All that one can say is that, if these barbarians leave no doubt that they are human, intelligent beings, it is because they have the form, the face, and the faculty of speech of human beings.[16]

Edwin James of the Long expedition, while admitting a considerable diversity of character among Plains Indians, argued that they all had traits common to a "race of barbarians," that "the shades of barbarism in which they are enveloped, uniformly exclude the light of civilization."[17] German naturalist Duke Paul of Württemberg characterized Omaha singing as a howling "in which the dogs and the wolves of the wilderness joined,"[18] while author Henry Brackenridge, in contrasting the dress of Arikara men and women, found an analogy in nature. "On seeing a warrior dressed in all this finery, walking with his wife, who was comparatively plain in her dress or ornaments," he noted, "I could not but think this was following the order of nature, as in the peacock, the stag, and almost all animals, the male is lavishly decorated, while the female is plain and unadorned."[19]

Observers who viewed the Indians as barbaric savages also believed them to be childish or child-like and to exhibit limited powers of abstract thinking or reasoning. In discussing the Mandans, Maximilian noted that they were "vain, and in this respect childish, like all savage nations."[20] Edwin Denig stated that Indians had a limited world view, that they had difficulty understanding motives of "charity, benevolence, or pity." The Fort Union trader concluded that "Indians seldom reason, they act on impulse."[21] Explorer Edwin James, who also suggested that western Indians had a limited ability for abstract thinking, did qualify his remarks by admitting that his impressions were most likely based on his interpreter's inability to converse intelligently in an Indian language.[22] It is obvious today that many similar nineteenth-century misconceptions were founded on communication failures, a limited understanding and appreciation of Indian culture, or blinding prejudice.

Fur men and travelers frequently made comparisons between civilization, savagery, culture, or barbarity. Such comparisons are not only relative, but are also emotionally charged. Whites generally had little appreciation or understanding of Indian culture, and many viewed Indians from the point of view of the nineteenth-century cult of Anglo-Saxon racial superiority, or similar racial theories. Civilization meant European civilization. Religion was synonymous with Christianity. They expected Indian adjustment to European values and standards — there was little talk of European accommodation to Indian values. The practical question was whether Indians could or would adapt to or accept European civilization; the ethical question, less frequently asked, was whether such a transformation was desirable.

A popular belief held that the advance of civilization doomed the Indian and his way of life to extinction. Those who viewed the Indians as little better than wild beasts agreed that Indians and civilization were incompatible. Even those who considered Indians potentially capable of adopting western civilization had seen many demoralized border Indians. Many became resigned that Indians would be given insufficient time to learn civilization's graces and virtues before its vices destroyed them.

If, as the noble-savage enthusiasts suggested, an Indian's best qualities were inherent in his natural state, and if he was happier in a state of innocence than burdened down with the responsibilities of knowledge, then his prospects of successfully adapting to civilization appeared bleak. George Catlin's solution was government intervention designed to preserve Indians in a national park setting:

> And what a splendid contemplation too, when one (who has travelled these realms, and can duly appreciate them) imagines them as they *might* in future be seen (by some great protecting policy of government) preserved in their pristine beauty and wildness, in a *magnificent park,* where the world could see for ages to come, the native Indian in his classic attire, galloping his wild horse, with sinewy bow, and shield and lance, amid the fleeting herds of elks and buffaloes. What a beautiful and thrilling specimen for America to preserve and hold up to the view of her refined citizens and the world, in future ages! A nation's Park, containing man and beast, in all the wild and freshness of their nature's beauty![23]

French trader Antoine-Pierre Tabeau argued tha the Upper Missouri tribes were incapable of reasoning or of formulating sophisticated religious ideas.[24] Maximilian of Wied, supporting pseudo-radial theories, ranked American Indians immediately after Caucasians in terms of intellectual capacity. The German scientist reasoned that "if man, in all his varieties, has not received from the Creator equally perfect faculties, I am, at least, convinced that, in this respect, the Americans are not inferior to the Whites."[25] Rudolph Friederich Kurz was optimistic about the Indian and civilization. He argued that Indians were pragmatic in accepting what they found to be "profitable or agreeable." He believed Indians would accept European civilization if only given a chance. Although many observers were convinced that association with frontiersmen — whom Kurz characterized as surpassing "the savages themselves in brutality and turbulence" — was detrimental, Duke Paul of Württemberg was convinced that prolonged contact with Whites had improved Indians' moral development and encouraged them to forego certain "barbarous practices."[26] At the opposite pole, Henry Brackenridge, writing of the Arikaras, argued that if Indians seemed to suffer in virtue from contacts with Whites, it was not because white behavior introduced any new vices, but because it presented "temptations which easily overcome those good qualities, 'which sit so loosely about them.' "[27]

Some traders believed that intermarriage would facilitate the Indian's passage toward civilization, yet many also held that mixed-bloods demonstrated the worst of both worlds.[28] Bellevue trader Pierre A. Sarpy's opinion is illustrative. In the course of an interview in the summer of 1860 with anthropologist Lewis Henry Morgan, a coarse Bellevue ferrymen paraphrased Sarpy's solution:

> He said old Col. Sarpey [sic] had the right view of the matter, and without quoting Col. Sarpey's [sic] language, . . . a short and energetic method of taming the Indian, which had a true French cast . . . was in substance that the only way to tame the Indian was to put white blood in his veins . . . I afterwards met Col. Peter A. Sarpy at Omaha and stated the ferryman's version of his remedy for the cure of the Red Man and he at once accepted it as correct. He said if you attempt to domesticate a wolf, he will snap at everything which comes near him, and do what you will he is always a wolf. So with the Indian. And the only way to tame him is to put in the white blood. He thought the government could not do a better thing than to send men among them for that purpose, etc. He was tight, I should say, at the time we had the conversation.

Although Morgan may have winced at the inebriated trader's crass expressions, he did agree that the idea had merit and he speculated that the general "improvement" in the Indian race might well be due to the white blood already "taken up" by Indian nations.[29]

A handful of traders reasoned that the Indian's demise would be of little consequence. Author Henry Brackenridge, who believed that "the savage state is contemplated to most advantage at a distance," pronounced judgment on the Arikaras: "The world would lose but little if these people should disappear before civilized communities."[30] Hudson's Bay trader Peter Skene Ogden, venting his bile at the Blackfeet on September 7 of 1825, wrote: "I wish to God all these Villains were burning in Hell if there be such a place."[31]

If an irritated trader, reflecting the cult of Anglo-Saxon racial superiority, could convince himself that Indians had few or no redeeming qualities, or if he envisioned their demise as having little economic or moral consequence, genocide might appear to be a logical course of action. In January of 1828 during a trying winter among the Snake Indians in Idaho, Ogden responded positively to the suggestion of two American trappers who were camped in the vicinity, that they declare war on the Snakes. Ogden was restrained by fear of violating company policy. "But as an individual acting for myself," he asserted, "I will not hesitate to say I would most willingly sacrifice a year and even two to exterminate the whole Snake tribe, women and children excepted, and in so doing I am of opinion [I] could fully Justify myself before God and man." In disarming possible critics, he concluded: "I full well know, those who live at a distance are of a different opinion, and the only reply I should make to them is, gentlemen, come, endure and suffer as we have done and Judge for yourselves, if forebearance and submission has not been carried too far, even beyond the bounds ordained by Scripture, and surely this is the only Guide that a Christian should follow."[32]

Traders and explorers did concede that Indians possessed many virtues. Kurz insisted that Indians displayed all of the basic human emotions of love, hate, sorrow, and joy, but reasoned that pride and stoicism made them more restrained than Whites in the expression of their feelings.[33] The fur-trade literature is filled with accounts of grief-stricken widows hacking off a finger as a sign of mourning, although observers were often repelled by the practice.[34] Edwin Denig considered the Crows' ability to settle domestic disputes without bloodshed as a truly remarkable quality.[35]

Whites were equally impressed by sensational feats of endurance. Pierre-Antoine Tabeau reported that the Arikaras thought nothing of walking "eighty or a hundred leagues . . . only to take the air."[36] Traders were also impressed with Indian horsemanship, swimming skills, and an apparently remarkable ability to withstand pain. Peter Skene Ogden described a man in 1827 who had amputated his own arm just below the armpit with a stone knife and a stone ax. In an understatement the trader allowed that the Indian must have suffered "considerable pain," and added that the fact that the wound had healed was nothing less than "incredible."[37] In 1823, Duke Paul observed that wounded Sioux bore up under pain with "patience and resignation." Traders also commented on Indians' ability to withstand adversity without complaint. Ogden, who frequently lamented his own wretched condition, admitted that the Snakes stoically withstood hunger better than Whites:

> What an example is this for us, when we are as at present for in-
> stance without Beaver and reduced to one meal a day how loudly
> and grieviously do we complain, but in truth how unjustly and
> without cause when I consider the Snakes sufferings compared
> to . . . ours[.] Many a day do they pass without food and still with-
> out a complaint or murmur and in this wretched manner do they
> pass their *lives*.[38]

Although George Catlin vehemently disagreed, most visitors to the High Plains complained about begging or theft. Most
were only at variance concerning which tribe harbored the
worst offenders. Edwin Denig observed that Crows were
especially expert in stealing small items from Whites, but admitted that they also victimized one another as readily. Pierre-
Antoine Tabeau complained that Poncas were the worst
thieves, while Maximilian and John Bradbury castigated the
Sioux, Assiniboine, Hidatsa, and Blackfeet. In fact, Maximilian
regarded begging as the "most troublesome habit of the
Blackfeet," although he conceded that they were less
troublesome in this respect than the Hidatsa.[39] Lewis Saum, in
The Fur Trader and the Indian, quotes ex-trader William Gordon as rationalizing that the only reason Crow Indians didn't
murder Whites was that if they did, the Whites might not
return, in which case "they would lose the chance of stealing
from us."[40]

Although traders often spoke of Indian hospitality and
generosity, it was clear that Indians expected reciprocity, an expectation that doubtless gave rise to the term "Indian giving."
During his residence among the Arikaras, Pierre-Antoine
Tabeau discovered that he could not afford to share their
hospitality at mealtime, because he would then be expected to
reciprocate in kind by feeding the entire tribe.[41] In August of
1833, Maximilian lamented at Fort McKenzie that Indian visits
to the post were so numerous and of such long duration that it
was impossible to procure the necessary food for them. "This is,
doubtless, a chief cause of the animosity of the Indians to the
Whites," the German prince observed.[42] It was primarily for
this reason that traders practiced reserve in their dealings with
Indians. Edwin James observed that in the course of conversation, western Indians tended to become "more and more
familiar and impertinent, till at length, their familiarity is succeeded by contempt and insult."[43] Traders such as Edwin Denig

34

refused to wear frontier clothing on the grounds that it might encourage familiarity and contempt. Rudolph Kurz reasoned that "generosity on the part of a paleface wins neither their friendship nor their respect." He used the following example:

> If one presented an Indian with a gift every day in the year — this morning, a horse; tomorrow, a gun; the day after tomorrow, a blanket; the next day, a knife; and so on until the last day in the year — and then might forget or simply neglect to give him anything at all on the 365th day, he would be all the more angry on account of the omission.[44]

Traders and travelers had ample opportunity to sample Indian cuisine and generally agreed upon two points. Most were repulsed by the filth associated with Indian culinary arts and were amazed by Indians' seeming ability to consume prodigious quantities of food. Duke Paul described a meal offered him in an Oto lodge which consisted of a freshly butchered dog and jerked bison. "This choice meal was boiled with corn in a kettle which for a considerable time had needed a good scouring. A most unappetizing horn spoon was used for skimming. Only the direst hunger and the utmost self-control," he concluded, "could have induced a European to have partaken of the food."[45] Paul's snowbound traveling companion of a later expedition, Balduin Mollhausen, after having been rescued from the wind-swept steppes of Nebraska by a hunting party of Otos in January 1852, expressed unbridled enthusiasm for his new vagabond existence, and for his rescuers, whom he regarded as gentle aborigines, as the personification of the noble savages who had inspired his wanderlust to America. "I felt in the most joyous spirits [he recalled], and seemed to be realizing the dreams of my youth (dreams conjured up certainly by Cooper and Washington Irving). . . . In the enthusiasm of such moments," he continued, "I do not think I would have changed places with any man on the whole earth! . . . I seemed to be overpaid for all my privations."[46] The Prussian was less enthusiastic about Oto cuisine. On one occasion, his hosts invited him to feast on one of the motley array of shaggy dogs in the camp. Mollhausen was forced to concede that dog meat was actually rather tasty to a man in his emaciated condition, but he argued that the meal might have been much more palatable if he had not been on such intimate terms with the dog before it had been thrown into the soup kettle.[47] Tabeau reported that "after having eaten almost a year with the Ricaras, one ought not to be allowed to be fastidious or disgusted,"[48] In an optimistic note, Edwin Denig concluded in his essay on the Sioux that "if a person could abstract the idea of filth, or the filth itself from their cooking, the food offered to strangers in their homes is good enough."[49]

American and European observers viewed Indian victuals as not only unclean, but often unwholesome. Some marveled that Indians did not suffer unpleasant consequences from some of their eating habits. In February 1834, Maximilian wrote from Fort Clark that the Mandans had discovered a dead buffalo cow in the prairie, and although it was partially decayed, "they greedily devoured it."[50] Fort Union Trader Edwin Denig noted with some aversion that Arikaras preferred the putrefied flesh of drowned buffalos found floating down the Missouri amid spring ice floes. The flesh was so decomposed, Denig noted, that "the meat will scarcely stick together, and can be eaten with a spoon in its raw state, yet these Indians devour it greedily, even when other and good meat can be had."[51] Duke Paul of Wurttemberg in 1823 complained that Omahas often ate tanned or dried skins, grasshoppers, and bark[52]. In 1826, Peter Skene Ogden reported on the table fare found in a Snake Indian hut:

> I had often heard these wretches subsisted on ants, Locusts and small fish in size not larger than minnies and I was determined to find out if it was not an exaggeration of late travellers, but to my surprise I found it was the case, for in one of their Dishes not of a small size filled with ants and ... Locusts [which] they collect in summer and store up for their winter, in eating they give the preference to the former being oily the latter not, on this food [if such it may be called] these poor wretches drag out an existence for nearly four months in the Year. . . .[53]

Gluttony was another popular topic of conversation. Tabeau argued that "the greatest and the true happiness of the Savages lies in gluttony. It is the subject of all their conversation, as it is the first object of their own interests, and, being incompatible with economy and caution, exposes them so often to distress and famine. They would always have more provisions than would be needed to sustain them, if they were not prodigal in times of abundance."[54] Here Tabeau raised the argument that Indian eating habits were symptomatic of their general improvidence about the future. Even George Catlin, who denied that Indians were "enormous eaters," admitted in writing of the Mandans that their inclinations were "solely directed to the enjoyment of the present day, without the sober reflections on the past or apprehensions of the future."[55] Kurz asserted that Indians' "highest efforts are put forth for pleasure of sense. . . . An Indian's ideal of enjoyment in the home is a feast; tobacco smoking is his diversion; dancing, his excess of indulgence in pleasure."[56]

Although there were important exceptions, most fur men and travelers believed that Indians had an insatiable craving for liquor, would do almost anything to obtain it, and had difficulty being temperate in its use. Typical was Maximilian's statement concerning the Blackfeet. He noted that "brandy is the greatest luxury of these Indians, as of all other North Americans, for which they will willingly part with everything they possess. . . . They will even offer their wives and children for sale in order to obtain it."[57]

Traders frequently complained that without liquor the trade did not flourish, and that no other trade article was so successful in inducing Indians to provide furs for the trade. Maximilian complained at Fort Union in June of 1833 that he could obtain very little from the Assiniboine in barter because brandy was always demanded in payment. Kurz quoted Edwin Denig's argument that the use of whisky in the trade would actually make Indians more reliable and industrious, "for the simple reason, universally accepted as true, that people work more diligently for their pleasures than for the necessities of life."[58]

Although there were ample accounts of Indians' unbridled passion for liquor, there was also a considerable body of contrary opinion. Edwin James doubted the veracity of such stories, attributing the use of liquor more to greedy fur traders than Indians' ungovernable appetites. George Catlin argued that North American Indians were the most temperate people he had ever encountered. Pierre-Antoine Tabeau, noted for his critical observations about the Arikaras, suggested that the introduction of intoxicating liquors in trade with Arikaras and Sioux would be useless. He quoted an unnamed Indian as saying, "Since you wish to laugh at my expense . . . you ought at least to pay me." Traders also universally agreed that Crows would not imbibe.[59]

Beginning with the first interactions between Englishmen and Indians in Virginia, Whites repeatedly commented on an apparent duality of Indian nature. On one hand, an Indian might demonstrate the virtues of bravery, honor, trustworthiness, endurance, or stoic detachment in the face of adversity — but he might also appear treacherous, cowardly, murderous, and thievish. What most trappers failed to mention, of course, was that duality is a characteristic of all human nature. Henry Brackenridge's characterization of the Arikaras is a case in point:

> They have amongst them their poor, their envious, their slanderers, their mean and crouching, their haughty and overbearing, their unfeeling and cruel, their weak and vulgar, their dissipated and wicked; and they have also, their brave and wise, their generous and magnanimous, their rich and hospitable, their pious and virtuous, their kind, frank, and affectionate, and in fact, all the diversity of characters that exists amongst the most refined people; but as their vices are covered by no veil of delicacy, their virtues may be regarded rather as the effect of involuntary impulse, than as the result of sentiment.[60]

Duke Paul of Württemberg, who saw more of the frontier in North and South America during the first half of the nineteenth century than did any other European traveler, was not only convinced of the duality of Indian nature, but was also of the opinion that the key to successful interaction was to demonstrate a Teutonic superiority and will of courageous resolution. During his first journey to North America in 1823, he observed that "the Indian in his natural state gives the psychologist a hard problem to solve, in the determination of his mental faculties. In many important moments of life, he appears thoughtful, resolute, firm, taciturn, and endowed with much moral strength, while he recoils weak and irresolute from things which seem unexplainable to him. . . ."[61]

Paul had ample opportunity to test this thesis during his subsequent intermittent travels in North America, spanning more than three decades. His rich and varied experiences among North American Indians gave him no cause to change his earlier opinions. His characterization of a hostile encounter with Pawnees near Fort Kearny in 1851 was typical of the attitudes held by many traders and fur men:

> Such Indians are always troublesome . . . but with travels such as mine [they] are one of the worst plagues and even highly dangerous, if one does not possess the most necessary tact and courageous resolve, which is so necessary for whites to have in confrontations with redskins in order to avoid their begging and

thievery. As chivalrous, as tough when hard pressed, as manly as the Indian can prove to be; in other cases . . . he is not ashamed of the most unmanly deed, he shows himself as womanish, even timid.

He added that "as they saw that I derided their threats, they showed themselves as cowardly as boys that look after baggage & unworthy to be called Indians." He concluded in contempt, "What a contrast between such a rabble and Cooper's Pawnees among *Hard Heart*.!"[62]

A common assumption held that the trader must not only present a bold front in the face of danger but that he must also punish Indians for any wrongdoing. Peter Skene Ogden would probably have had the support of many of his fellow traders had they read the following statement which he penned in his journal in February of 1827. After lamenting his losses at the hands of the Snakes, he detailed what he considered an ideal mode of Indian diplomacy: "Altho [sic] it may appear so to those who reside at a distance free from the anxiety and care that an Indian Trador or Conductor of Trappers is subject to, a cruel mode,[,] but I am of opinion if on first discovering a strange Tribe a dozen of them were shot it would be the means of preserving many lives which in the course of four or five years are lost by Indians.[63]

Virtually all travelers in Indian country were men. Many were young and virile. Most commented on the relation between the sexes, the status of women, and sexual mores. Although travelers frequently found Indian women both beautiful and exotic, they usually rated men much higher than women in terms of grace and handsome physical characteristics. This was due in large measure to the fact that women did menial labor. Their occupation of cooking and dressing skins often left them greasy and dirty. Women appeared decidedly drab when compared to travelers' and traders' descriptions of their male counterparts. Whites never failed to be impressed by Plains Indian men. Most observers agreed that men of the Crow nation were the best dressed and most handsome of the Upper Missouri tribes. Edwin Denig argued that they were "decidedly prepossessing in their appearance," that "the warrior class is perhaps the handsomest body of Indians in North America," and "as far as outward appearance goes, are much the finest looking of all the tribes." Catlin termed them "fine looking and noble gentlemen . . . a handsome and well-formed set of men as can be seen in any part of the world. . . . No tribe of Indians on the Continent are better able to produce a pleasing and thrilling effect," the artist continued, for "they may be justly said to be the most beautifully clad of all the Indians in these regions. . . ."[64] It is not surprising that Plains Indians have become the symbol of the North American Indian.[65]

Relations between the sexes proved to be a lively topic of animated discussion. Writers were fascinated by what they viewed as departures from accepted convention, and devoted considerable space to the subject in their journals and diaries. Traders often pointed out that Indian men seemed to practice a double standard. They might offer a traveler a wife or sister as a gesture of hospitality, or might sell her favors in exchange for trade goods. As punishment for infidelity, however, he might cut off her nose, a form of mutilation commonly observed on the Upper Missouri during the first half of the nineteenth century. Traders frequently failed to mention their own double standard of sexual morality. Whites were often willing participants, yet they seldom expressed any indignation about their own part in these transactions.

Of all the tribes on the Upper Missouri, the Arikaras seem to have come in for the most criticism. Naturalist John Bradbury recorded how eagerly Arikaras offered their wives' favors for trade goods, and how they found a ready market among the expedition's Canadian employees: "In this species of liberality no nation can exceed the Aricaras, who flocked down every evening with their wives, sisters, and daughters, anxious to meet with a market for them. The Canadians were very good customers, and Mr. Hunt was kept in full employ during the evening, in delivering out to them blue beads and vermillion, the articles in use for this kind of traffic.[66]

Bradbury's contemporary and friend, Henry Brackenridge, discussed the virtues of self-control in the midst of such temptations, while adding the following footnote to this illicit trade: "The silly boatmen, in spite of the endeavors of the leaders of our parties, in a short time disposed of almost every article which they possessed, even their blankets, and shirts. One of them actually returned to the camp, one morning entirely naked, having disposed of his last shirt — this might truly be called *la derniere chemisse de l'amour*." Brackenridge continued, "Seeing the chief one day in a thoughtful mood, I asked him what was the matter. 'I was wondering,' the Indian responded, 'whether you white people have any women amongst you.' I assured him in the affirmative," Brackenridge retorted. 'Then,' the chief asked, 'why is it that your people are so fond of our women, one might suppose they had never seen any before.'

Even Brackenridge admitted that such scenes were "by no means universal."[67]

There is probably no other topic about which fur men and western travelers had more to say than Indian warfare. Warfare interrupted the normal flow of furs and was economically detrimental to the trade. Traders occasionally attempted the difficult balancing act of maintaining simultaneous trade relations between two warring tribes, but found their attempts both difficult and dangerous. Traders frequently longed for a general peace, but experience convinced many that Indians were incapable of maintaining peace for any length of time. Edwin Denig described warfare as the essence of the Indian way of life. "Indians to be Indians must have war," he stated. "Next to the chase," Maximilian agreed, "war is the chief employment of the Indians, and military glory the highest object of their ambition." Kurz asserted that "the highest aim of an Indian brave is glory in war; accordingly there is perpetual hostility among the different tribes," while Tabeau characterized Indian warfare as "the greatest plague of all the Savages of the Upper Missouri."[68]

Conclusion

The picture which emerges from the accounts of nineteenth-century traders and travelers is difficult to assess. In the first place, documentation is limited. A vast majority of fur men left no written records at all of their experiences among the Indians. Many who kept diaries or wrote correspondence were primarily concerned with economic or commercial affairs and made only peripheral mention of Indians. Opinions expressed in some travel narratives were based upon superficial exposure and contain little analysis. Accounts frequently contradict one another. Many travelers had problems communicating through interpreters. It is not surprising that interpreters with limited education or little sophistication were unable to adequately translate complicated ideas or concepts. Traders frequently wrote highly critical statements and abusive rhetoric under extreme provocation, irritation, or under trying conditions. These statements may not accurately reflect a fur man's basic attitude under more normal circumstances. There is also a problem of selectivity. Authors of travel narratives were prone to stress the exotic, the unusual, or the sensational. Few concentrated on the more mundane aspects of Indian life. Some made sweeping and often stereotyped generalizations based on limited observation.

Many traders' views were clouded by economic considerations. Whether a character trait seemed good or bad in a fur man's judgment might be closely tied to whether it was beneficial or detrimental to the trade. Yet regardless of criticism, Indians were an integral part of the trade; traders, regardless of their views, were eager to trade with them. However, the gulf between cultures was too great to facilitate understanding or sympathy. Ethnocentric attitudes made it difficult for Whites not to be critical of cultures, world views, or life styles which differed markedly from their own. Many were blinded by their own preconceptions. It is therefore not surprising that written accounts tended to be critical and that fur men and travelers seemed to extol few virtues while decrying what they considered to be manifold vices among the Indians.

Notes

[1] William H. Goetzmann, *Exploration and Empire: The Explorer and the Scientist in the Winning of the American West* (New York: Alfred A. Knopf, 1966), p. 181.

[2] Rudolph Friederich Kurz, *The Journal of Rudolph Friederich Kurz: The Life and Work of this Swiss Artist* (Fairfield: Ye Galleon Press, 1969), pp. 1-2.

[3] George Catlin, *Letters and Notes on the Manners, Customs, and Condition of the North American Indians*, 2 vols. (New York: Dover, 1973), 1:9.

[4] Kurz, *Journal*, p. 2.

[5] Henry M. Brackenridge, *Journal of a Voyage up the Missouri River Performed in Eighteen Hundred and Eleven*, vol. VI of *Early Western Travels, 1784-1897*, ed. Ruben Gold Thwaites, 32 vols., (Cleveland: Arthur H. Clark, 1904-1907), p. 119.

[6] Kurz, *Journal*, p. 35, 224.

[7] *Ibid.*, pp. 45-46.

8 *Ibid.*, pp. 38, 130.

9 Catlin, *Letters and Notes*, 1:2.

10 Kurz, *Journal*, p. 87.

11 *Ibid.*, p. 352.

12 Catlin, *Letters and Notes*, 1:10, 23, 46-47, 84-85, 205.

13 Kurz, *Journal*, pp. 39, 82.

14 Peter Skene Ogden, *Traits of American Indian Life and Character* (San Francisco: The Grabhorn Press, 1933), Introduction. Ogden's attitudes toward Indians are examined in depth in David E. Miller, "Peter Skene Ogden Discovered Indians," in *Charles Reed Monographs in Western History, No. 3, Essays on the American West 1972-1973*, ed. by Thomas G. Alexander (Provo: Brigham Young University Press, 1974), pp. 137-166.

15 Maximilian Alexander of Wied-Neuwied, *Travels in the Interior of North America*, vols. 22-25 of *Early Western Travels, 1784-1897*, ed. Ruben Gold Thwaites, 32 vols.; (Cleveland: Arthur H. Clark, 1904-1907), 23:41, 91.

16 Pierre-Antoine Tabeau, *Tabeau's Narrative of Loisel's Expedition to the Upper Missouri*, ed. Annie Heloise Abel (Norman: University of Oklahoma Press, 1939), p. 172.

17 Edwin James, *Account of an Expedition from Pittsburgh to the Rocky Mountains*, 3 vols. (Philadelphia, 1823), 2:376.

18 Duke Paul Wilhelm von Württemberg, *Travels in North America, 1822-1824*, ed. Savoie Lottinville (Norman: University of Oklahoma Press, 1973), p. 340.

19 Brackenridge, *Journal*, p. 121.

20 Maximilian, *Travels*, 23:258.

21 Edwin Denig as quoted in Lewis O. Saum, *The Fur Trader and the Indian* (Seattle: University of Washington Press, 1965), p. 145; Edwin Denig, *Five Indian Tribes of the Upper Missouri: Sioux, Arickaras, Assiniboines, Crees, Crows*, ed. John C. Ewers (Norman: University of Oklahoma Press, 1961), p. 171.

22 James, *Expedition*, 2:368-369.

23 Catlin, *Letters and Notes*, 1:261-262.

24 Tabeau, *Narrative*, p. 190.

25 Maximilian, *Travels*, 23:284.

26 Kurz, *Journal*, p. 361-362; Paul von Württemberg, *Travels*, p. 381. Paul had equal distaste for "the descendants of many white Europeans who live near them and whose crudeness often exceeds the bounds of decency." *Ibid.*, p. 385.

27 Brackenridge, *Journal*, pp. 128-129.

[28] See Saum, *The Fur Trader and the Indian*, p. 206.

[29] Lewis Henry Morgan, *The Indian Journals, 1859-1862, of Lewis Henry Morgan*, ed. Leslie A. White (Ann Arbor: University of Michigan, 1959), pp. 93-94.

[30] Brackenridge, *Journal*, p. 128.

[31] Peter Skene Ogden, *Peter Skene Ogden's Snake Country Journals, 1824-25 and 1825-26*, ed. E. E. Rich (London: Hudson's Bay Record Society, 1950), p. 79.

[32] Peter Skene Ogden, *Peter Skene Ogden's Snake Country Journals, 1827-28 and 1828-29*, ed. Glyndwr Williams (London: The Hudson's Bay Record Society, 1971), pp. 51-52.

[33] Kurz, *Journal*, p. 221.

[34] See Maximilian, *Travels*, 23:121, 362; Denig, *Five Indian Tribes*, pp. 157-158; Catlin, *Letters and Notes*, 1:90; Duke Paul von Wurttemberg, *Travels*, pp. 319-320; Tabeau, *Narrative*, pp. 191-192; and John Bradbury, *Travels in the Interior of America, 1809-11*, vol. 5 of *Early Western Travels, 1784-1897*, ed. Ruben Gold Thwaites, 32 vols. (Cleveland; Arthur H. Clark, 1904-1907), p. 115.

[35] Denig, *Five Indian Tribes*, pp. 150-152.

[36] Tabeau, *Narrative*, p. 173.

[37] Peter Skene Ogden, *Peter Skene Ogden's Snake Country Journal, 1826-27*, ed. by K. G. Davies (London: Hudson's Bay Record Society, 1961), p. 74; Duke Paul von Wurttemberg, *Travels*, p. 369.

[38] Ogden, *Snake Country Journal, 1826-1827*, p. 21.

[39] Catlin, *Letters and Notes*, 1:210; Denig, *Five Indian Tribes*, p. 153; Tabeau, *Narrative*, pp. 100-101; Maximilian, *Travels*, 22:360-363; 23:12, 112, 161, 163; 24:47.

[40] Saum, *The Fur Trader and the Indian*, p. 140.

[41] Tabeau, *Narrative*, p. 145.

[42] Maximilian, *Travels*, 23:111-112.

[43] James, *Expedition*, 2:372.

[44] Kurz, *Journal*, pp. 154-155.

[45] Duke Paul, *Travels*, p. 384.

[46] Balduin Möllhausen, *Diary of a Journey from the Mississippi to the Coasts of the Pacific with a United States Government Expedition*, trans., Mrs. Percy Sinnett, 2 vols. (London: Longmans, Brown & Green, 1858), 1:210.

[47] *Ibid.*, p. 200.

[48] Tabeau, *Narrative*, p. 174.

[49] Denig, *Five Indian Tribes*, p. 50.

[50] Maximilian, *Travels*, 24:70.

[51] Denig, *Five Indian Tribes*, p. 49.

[52] Duke Paul, *Travels*, p. 367.

[53] Ogden, *Snake Country Journals, 1824-1825 and 1825-1826*, pp. 133-134.

[54] Tabeau, *Narrative*, pp. 207-208.

[55] Catlin, *Letters and Notes*, 1:85, 123.

[56] Kurz, *Journal*, pp. 152, 227.

[57] Maximilian, *Travels*, 23:109.

[58] *Ibid.*, p. 17; Kurz, *Journal*, pp. 176-177.

[59] James, *Expedition*, 2:374; Catlin, *Letters and Notes*, 1:210; Tabeau, *Narrative*, p. 171.

[60] Brackenridge, *Journal*, p. 128.

[61] Duke Paul, *Travels*, pp. 380-381.

[62] Duke Paul von Wurttemberg entry for November 2, 1851, Ms Diary in possession of author. Trans. by D. H. Miller.

[63] Ogden, *Snake Country Journal, 1826-27*, p. 71.

[64] Denig, *Five Indian Tribes*, pp.154-155; Catlin, *Letters and Notes*, 1:49, 192.

[65] See John C. Ewers, "The Emergence of the Plains Indian as a Symbol of the North American Indian," in *Indian Life on the Upper Missouri* (Norman, University of Oklahoma Press, 1968), pp. 187-203.

[66] Bradbury, *Travels*, pp. 134.

[67] Brackenridge, *Journal*, pp. 130-131.

[68] Denig, *Five Indian Tribes*, p. 62; Maximilian, *Travels*, 23:348; Kurz, *Journal*, p. 350; Tabeau, *Narrative*, p. 204.

Changing Concepts:
The Indians Learn About the "Long Knives" and Settlers (1849-1890s)

Donald J. Berthrong, Purdue University

Until the mid-nineteenth century, the Great Plains Indians flourished in a generous environment. The Great Plains were still relatively free from white intruders, there was room enough for all of the tribes, while the buffalo and other game provided food for the tribes of the plains, prairies and mountains. Over the Platte River and Santa Fe roads, traders and emigrants passed through the Great Plains to a rendezvous with mountain men, to the Pacific Coast or to Santa Fe. Until the Treaty of Guadalupe Hidalgo of 1848, the trickle of commerce and travel did not endanger either Indian lands or the buffalo herds. Indications were present, however, that when commercial and emigrant traffic increased, there would be conflict. Along the Santa Fe Trail during the 1820s, there was sporadic fighting between freighters, troops, and Indians with occasional death to Whites or Indians. The flow of goods and people, nevertheless, was rarely interrupted until the 1860s. One historian of the Platte River Road maintains that until that decade, there is no verifiable Indian attack upon an emigrant train. Some 350,000 people moved westward over the Platte River Road until it was replaced by railroads, and except for the period after 1863, the emigrants traveled in comparative safety.[1]

Indian orators insist with unanimity that the Plains Indians did not initiate the White-Indian wars. Ten Bears of the Comanches, whose life spanned the early years of the Santa Fe Trail and the conflicts of the 1860s, reminded government negotiators at the 1867 Treaty of Medicine Lodge that his people "have never first drawn a bow or fired a gun against the Whites. There has been trouble on the line between us, . . . but it was not begun by us. It was you who sent out the first soldier, and it was we who sent out the second. . . ."[2] Red Cloud, the renowned Oglala leader, recalled that at the 1851 Treaty of Fort Laramie, his people pledged to allow soldiers and travelers to pass through their country for 55 years. "We kept our word," Red Cloud asserted, "we committed no murders, no depredations, until the troops came here. When the troops were sent, then trouble and disturbance arose." The Oglala leader also reminded a white audience that the Sioux were not belligerent toward civilians: "Ask any one who has gone through to California. They will tell you we have treated them well."[3]

The California- and Oregon-bound emigrants did cause problems to the Indians. Washakie, the principal chief of the Shoshones, whose country lay west of the Great Plains, lamented as early as 1855 that "this country was once covered with buffalo, elk, deer, and antelope, and we had plenty to eat, and also robes for bedding, and to make lodges. But now, since the white man has made a road across our land, and has killed off our game, we are hungry, and there is nothing for us to eat. Our women and children cry for food and we have no food to give them."[4] What was true among the Shoshones was also undoubtedly true for Sioux bands living near the Platte River Road. Hunger caused uneasiness among the Indians, and conflicts arose in 1854 between United States troops and the Sioux.

In 1849, a garrison had been sent to Fort Laramie to protect travelers to the Pacific Coast. By the summer of 1853, the soldiers of the garrison and Sioux warriors were spoiling for a fight. A detachment of soldiers from the fort attempted to arrest a warrior who had shot at a soldier-ferryman on the North Platte River. Only the influence of the chiefs kept the Brulés, Oglalas, and Miniconjous from retaliating for the deaths of six warriors at the hands of the detachment. More than a year later, on August 18, 1854, a Mormon emigrant appeared at Fort Laramie, complaining that an Indian had appropriated one of his cattle for food. Conquering Bear, chief of the Miniconjous, tried to placate the Whites with a promise that restitution would be made when treaty goods came to Fort Laramie. The inexperienced officer in charge of the fort and his subordinate, Brevet Second Lieutenant John L. Grattan, however, thought that it was time to intimidate the Sioux living in the vicinity of Fort Laramie.

Lt. Grattan boasted that with his detachment of thirty, supported by a howitzer and a mountain gun, he could whip the Sioux. At Conquering Bear's village, a parley failed to produce the young Miniconjou who had killed the Mormon's cow. Losing patience, Lt. Grattan ordered his artillery to fire upon the village. Conquering Bear was mortally wounded from small arms fire, but Miniconjou, Brulé, and Oglala warriors killed the whole detachment.[5] The incident substantially changed the Indians' perceptions about the trustworthiness of troops. The ease with which the soldiers had been killed emboldened the Indians to run off stock from emigrants and waylay a Salt Lake City stage, killing three and wounding another. Throughout the United States, demands were strong for revenge for the killing of Grattan's command and for protection of travelers over the Platte River and Santa Fe roads. By the end of 1854, fifty-two forts ringed the Plains from Texas to the Upper Missouri River, each post a potential trouble spot if Indian warriors and troops did not sublimate desires to strike their foes.[6]

The challenge to the Plains warriors did not come from garrison soldiers. To deal with the Sioux, Colonel William S. Harney, a veteran of the Black Hawk and Seminole wars, assembled an expedition at Fort Kearny, consisting of infantry, dragoons, and artillery. Harney believed that Indians should be chastized before peace councils occurred, proclaiming as his 600-man column marched out of Fort Kearny on August 24, 1855, "By God, I'm for battle — no peace." Little Thunder's Brulés were in Harney's path at Ash Hollow on the north bank of the North Platte River, and supposedly all non-belligerent Sioux were concentrated south of that river. Although Little Thunder's village contained some of the young men responsible for 1854-1855 winter raids, the chief did not consider himself unfriendly to Whites. Locating the Brulé village, Harney divided his command above and below the camp, and parleyed with Little Thunder, demanding that the troublemakers be surrendered. Failing to obtain the young warriors, Harney's infantry moved in and opened fire on the tipis. Dragoons charged into the camp from above, scattering the panicked Brules. Cut off from easy flight, the Brulés were slaughtered — less than one-half of the villagers escaped death or imprisonment.

Harney marched on to Fort Laramie. There he insisted

that the warriors responsible for the Salt Lake City mail coach attack be surrendered. Since too few Sioux were at Fort Laramie, no peace council occurred, and Harney marched through the heart of Sioux country to the Missouri River at Fort Pierre, challenging the Sioux nation. Fearful for the safety of the women and children seized at Ash Hollow and imprisoned at Fort Kearny, the Sioux allowed Harney to complete his sweep. Reportedly, on October 25, 1855, Spotted Tail, Red Leaf, and Long Chin, who had participated in the attack on the Salt Lake City stage surrendered; they were imprisoned at Fort Leavenworth for one year. Thereafter, Spotted Tail consistently counseled for peace with the white men. Assuming treaty-making powers, Harney in March of 1856 dictated peace terms to representatives of the Teton Sioux. The Sioux chiefs promised to keep the peace and agreed to accept a tribal government led by chiefs and sub-chiefs who were to be appointed by Harney and who henceforth would be responsible for hostile actions taken by their warriors.[7]

On the central Plains, the Cheyennes were the next objective of the Army. At the Upper Platte Bridge in April 1856, Captain Henry Heth had attempted to arrest three young Cheyennes over the disputed ownership of a horse. During the fracas, one Cheyenne was killed and another wounded. In another incident, while looking for Pawnees in the summer of 1856, a Cheyenne war party killed a traveler near Fort Kearny and defiantly rode into the fort. Captain Henry W. Wharton tried and failed to seize three of the warriors as hostages. Piqued at his failure, Captain Wharton, after a mail coach driver had come to the fort with an arrow sticking into his arm, struck a camp of about 80 Cheyennes, killing 10 and wounding many more. Cheyenne retaliations along the Platte River Road followed, but Indian Agent Thomas Twiss persuaded the Cheyenne chiefs to withdraw.

Colonel Edwin V. Sumner was instructed to punish the Cheyennes. In July 1857, Colonel Sumner pushed into the buffalo ranges on the headwaters of the Solomon and Republican Rivers. Late that month, the Cheyennes and Sumner's cavalry confronted each other. Before the sabers of the 1st Cavalry, the Cheyennes fled the field. Only nine warriors and two troopers died of battle wounds, but Sumner's charge caused the Cheyennes and Arapahoes to cease their hostilities until the 1860s.[8]

From the 1840s onward, the Kiowas and Comanches raided the Texas frontier, avoiding hostilities in the Arkansas Valley and on the Santa Fe Trail. In Texas, however, the Kiowas and Comanches consistently skirmished with garrisons, the Texas Rangers, and the U.S. Cavalry. Finally, on May 11, 1858, Captain John S. (Rip) Ford, with 100 Texas Rangers and an equal number of Indian auxiliaries, surprised a large Comanche camp near the Antelope Hills on the South Canadian River. Ford's Rangers and auxiliaries routed 300 warriors, killing 78 and destroying the village. The Comanches then struck hard at the Santa Fe Trail, which led to another force being sent out in search of them. Major Earl Van Dorn attacked Buffalo Hump's 120 lodges near Rush Springs, Indian Territory, although the chief thought his people were safe following earlier peace overtures at Fort Arbuckle. Other search forays took the field against the Kiowas and Comanches, but Texans suffered intensely for Ford's and Van Dorn's attacks. Through 1860, Kiowas and Comanches had brushes with U.S. Cavalry units on the central and southern Plains.[9]

The military expeditions of the 1850s changed the Indians' perceptions of "long knives." Early infantry garrisons did not disturb the Plains warriors because they were incapable of pursuing a mounted, mobile people. Also, the garrisons were so weak that they could easily be crushed. Traders and Indian service personnel were likewise no threat, because they resided in Indian country at the leave of the tribes. Harney's, Sumner's, Ford's, and Van Dorn's columns were another matter. Combined infantry, cavalry, and artillery were too powerful for one band or tribe to defeat. Indians learned also that the army expeditions did not differentiate between friend or antagonist. If the opportunity arose, soldiers would kill Indian women and children, something that a warrior would not do except in a frenzy of retaliation. The Sioux also learned that soldiers caused factionalism within the tribes. Spotted Tail, for example, gathered about him people who would not fight again, which caused much consternation among the Brulés and ultimately led to the chief's death at the hands of Crow Dog.

During the era of the Civil War, the potential for White-Indian conflict escalated. Mining activity increased throughout the West but particularly on the edges of the Plains in Colorado and Montana. Miners, stage station operators, ranchers, farmers, merchants, and townspeople — all of whom required food, clothing, equipment, and land — moved in. Traffic along the established roads grew, and new thoroughfares such as the Bozeman, Smoky Hill, and South Platte Roads began to resemble an interconnected web through the Indians' country and buffalo ranges.

The Cheyennes were the first to protest. Their vast domain on the central Plains between the Arkansas and Platte Rivers had melted away to an insignificant and barren tract of land in southeastern Colorado Territory — the Sand Creek Reservation. The ambition of territorial officials for statehood and the unpleasantness of settlers drove the Cheyenne warriors to reprisals which led directly to the Sand Creek Massacre. The senseless butchery of Black Kettle's and White Antelope's Cheyenne and Arapaho people at Sand Creek on November 29, 1864, resulted in three years of conflict — really eleven years, if the Red River War is included as a continuation of the drive to pen the Cheyennes and Arapahoes on a reservation.

Black Kettle of the Cheyennes reflects the hesitancy of Plains Indian leaders to accept peace terms dictated by treaty commissioners who were supported by the "long knives" of the Great White Father. To the white treaty commissioners at the mouth of the Little Arkansas on October 12, 1865, Black Kettle complained: "Your young soldiers, I don't think they listen to you. You bring presents, and when I come to get them, I am afraid they will strike me before I get away. When I come in to receive presents I take them up crying. . . . I once thought that I was the only man that persevered to be the friend of the white man, but since they have come and cleaned out (robbed) our lodges, horses, and everything else, it is hard for me to believe white men any more. . . . All my friends — the Indians that are holding back — they are afraid to come in; . . . [they] are afraid they will be betrayed as I have been. I am not afraid of white men, but come and take you by the hand, and am glad to have an opportunity of so doing."[10] At the same council, Little Raven, the principal chief of the Arapahoes, joined Black Kettle in denouncing the soldiers: "There is something very strong for us — that fool band of soldiers that cleared out our lodges, and killed our women and children. This is very strong (hard) on us. There, at Sand Creek, is one chief, Left Hand; White Antelope and many other chiefs lie there; our women and children lie there. Our lodges were destroyed there, and our horses were taken from us there, and I do not feel disposed to go right off in a new country and leave them."[11]

The Treaty of the Little Arkansas and that of Fort Sully with the Sioux brought no peace to the Plains. Prior to the councils at Fort Sully in October of 1865, the Oglala and Miniconjou had blunted the sweep of General Patrick E. Conner's 2,500-man column into the Powder River country. At issue was the Bozeman Road which cut through the heart of the Powder River buffalo range to the Montana Territory mining camps. The Sioux remembered only too well how travelers along the Platte River and the protecting garrisons had destroyed the hunting ranges adjacent to that road. On the Bozeman Road, there were three forts — Reno, Phil Kearny, and C. F. Smith — in addition to Fort Fetterman that was located at the juncture of the Platte River and Bozeman Roads. Early in the summer of 1866 at Fort Laramie, Commissioner E. B. Taylor had attempted to ensnare prominent Teton Sioux chiefs into accepting the forts and the Bozeman Road. Red Cloud of the Oglalas understood the duplicity of the government: "The Great Father," Red Cloud said, "sends us presents and wants us to sell him the road but White Chief [Colonel Henry B. Carrington] goes with soldiers to steal the road before Indians say Yes or No." Leaving the Fort Laramie councils, the Oglalas, Miniconjous, Sans Arcs, Brulés, Cheyennes, and Arapahoes coalesced to cut the Bozeman Road and drive off the protecting garrisons.[12]

Shortly, civilian travel along the Bozeman Road was interdicted. Between July 26 and December 21, 1866, the Sioux had killed 5 officers, 91 enlisted men, and 58 civilians and had run off 771 head of stock.[13] Centering their assaults around Fort Phil Kearny, the Sioux and their allies badly defeated troops; on one occasion, they wiped out a detachment led by Captain William J. Fetterman. Better weapons enabled the beleaguered troops in 1867 to fight off large forces of warriors at the Wagon Box and the Hayfield fights. For nearly two years, Sioux leaders cut travel over the Bozeman Road to military wagon trains. Even after the Treaty of Fort Laramie in May 1868, Red Cloud remained obdurate, refusing to sign any document until the Bozeman Road had been cleared of troops. He informed the treaty commissioners: "When we see the soldiers moving away and the forts abandoned, then I will come down and talk."[14] Shortly after the troops were withdrawn from the forts, Red Cloud's warriors burned Forts Phil Kearny and C. F. Smith. Skirmishes continued around the other posts for another month. Finally, on November 6, 1868, Red Cloud came to Fort Laramie and placed his mark on the Treaty of Fort Laramie.

Red Cloud and the Sioux were temporarily successful in protecting the Powder River buffalo ranges. The 1860s mark the high tide of Indian resistance to white penetration of the Great Plains. Thereafter, the establishment of reservations ringed by military posts turned those tracts into prisons without walls. Although he believed that he had been deceived, Red Cloud fought no more. Two years after signing the Treaty of Fort Laramie, Red Cloud told a New York City audience: "In 1868 men came out and brought papers. We could not read them and they did not tell us what was in them. We thought the treaty was to remove the forts, and that we should then cease fighting. But they wanted to send us traders on the Missouri. We did not want to go to the Missouri, but wanted traders where we were. When I reached Washington, the Great Father explained to me what the treaty was, and showed me that the interpreters had deceived me. All I want is right and justice. . . . I represent the whole Sioux nation, and they will be bound by what I say. I am no Spotted Tail, to say one thing one day and be bought for a pin the next. Look at me, I am poor and naked, but I am the Chief of the nation."[15] With those words, Red Cloud went to his reservation, but Sioux leadership passed to Crazy Horse, Gall, and other warrior chiefs — who would destroy Custer's command on the Little Big Horn on June 25, 1876. Red Cloud's reputation among his own people eroded away as they forgot his heroism and victories on the Powder River.

On the Southern Plains during the winter of 1874-1875 and on the Northern Plains two winters later, Indian resistance to military campaigns ceased. Only Sitting Bull remained defiant in Canada, refusing to accept the inevitable decay of reservation life. Mutual respect among Indian warriors and white soldiers did not emerge from the wars for the Great Plains. Although extreme, Lt. Colonel George A. Custer, four years before his death, reflected the white soldier's view of the Plains warriors when he wrote: "We see him as he is, . . . a savage in every sense of the word; not worse, perhaps, than his white brother would be similarly born and bred, but one whose cruel and ferocious nature far exceeds that of any wild beast of the desert. That this is true no one who had been brought into intimate contact with the wild tribes will deny."[16]

Indian warriors and chiefs did not forget the Army's

strikes against their people. Colonel Harney was remembered by the Sioux as "The Butcher," Colonel Chivington's volunteers were called "those fool soldiers," Colonel Carrington's men were likened to thieves, and the Southern Cheyennes felt no sympathy for Custer when he died on the Little Big Horn. The more than occasional mutilation of fallen troopers indicated this disrespect, if not contempt, and the furious resentment accumulated by warriors during the conflicts on the Plains. Perhaps men of different cultures, goaded on by the barbarism of two decades of warfare, can never embrace in friendship the killers of their comrades or families.

Once the reservation system began to operate, warriors and garrison soldiers eyed each other warily. Soldiers became jailers; warriors became virtual prisoners, a condition hardly conducive to pleasant relationships. Fractious Indians found themselves in the post guardhouse living on short rations and seeking frantically a way to escape the stench of the cell. Reservation Indians became objects of profit to post traders; Indian women became temporary wives of enlisted men who simply left their spouses and their mixed-blood children when orders came to move to another post. Gamblers and horse race touts bilked Indians of their money and possessions, Indian women were prostituted, and rot-gut liquor flowed freely into the Indian camps — if Indian agency records are even faintly accurate. About the agency headquarters and the nearby army post, shabby towns inhabited by the scum of the frontier grew despite the opposition of the occasional conscientious Indian agent. These settlements served as deplorable, transitory stages to the legalized occupation of Indian reservations, brought about by the 1887 Dawes Act.

Indians learned during the reservation and allotment periods that white settlers' law, in part, controlled their lives. Major crimes became federal offenses after the historic Supreme Court case of *Crow Dog*. As a warrior, Crow Dog acted according to the customs of his culture when he killed Spotted Tail in 1881. In Crow Dog's mind, Spotted Tail had usurped the chieftainship of the Brulés and had brought disrepute to his tribe by his private and public deeds. Crow Dog was convicted of murder in the Territorial courts of Dakota and was sentenced to death.[17] Before the sentence was carried out, Crow Dog requested permission to visit his wife and sons. Accompanied by a deputy sheriff, Crow Dog rode to the Brulé agency headquarters where the deputy remained while the warrior traveled on to his village. The white officer became concerned when Crow Dog did not return to the agency on the appointed day. Indian police were dispatched to bring Crow Dog in, but Crow Dog's wife told the Indian police that her husband preferred to ride back to Rapid City alone. From the jail came a telegram "Crow Dog has just reported here."[18] The Brulé warrior had redeemed his honor and pledged to return to his captors, not suspecting that he would later be freed when the United States Supreme Court ruled that an Indian could not be tried in white courts for crimes committed against other Indians in Indian country.

In 1890, two Northern Cheyenne men killed a young white man named Hugh Boyle. Head Chief and Young Mule took refuge in their village at the Lame Deer agency, Montana Territory. Their relatives and friends offered to strip themselves of ponies and possessions "to cover" the crime and death of Boyle, but the offer was rejected by the Indian agent. Conviction of murder called for execution by hanging, a death which prevented a man's spirit from leaving the corpse. The Northern Cheyenne chiefs neither denied the crime nor defended their young men's action. They did, however, resist any effort to seize the young men so that they could be tried and hanged. It was finally determined that Head Chief and Young Mule would duel with a troop of cavalry. On September 13, 1890, after preparing themselves to die, Head Chief and Young Mule charged the dismounted troopers who slew them by gunfire. Neither of the men considered flight or the life of an outcast acceptable, and they died believing that their spirits would at least be free since they had paid in full for their indiscretion.[19]

Sometimes, when an Indian was unjustly accused of crime, he chose not to resist imprisonment. Cosah Red Lodge, a 26-year-old Cheyenne, was accused in June 1895 of raping an old white woman near Arapahoe, Oklahoma Territory. Indian Agent A. E. Woodson and the white citizens assumed that Red Lodge was guilty. Neighbors of the woman offered Red Lodge's jailor money and a pony if the Cheyenne would be delivered to them, but the sheriff maintained custody of his prisoner. Since Arapahoe had no jail, the sheriff, finding a baseball game attractive, took Red Lodge with him to the contest. To guard and protect Red Lodge, the sheriff deputized a number of men to guard him. Seeing Red Lodge, the crowd surged forward eager to kill him. Rather than have the mob descend upon him, the

Cheyenne motioned the deputies to shoot him. Red Lodge, who could not speak or understand English, acted out the role of a warrior. By signs he told the officers to kill him by pointing to his head and chest. As Red Lodge jumped from the buggy, the sheriff emptied his sixshooter at Red Lodge but missed. The Cheyenne then ran toward the mob, still trying to find someone who could kill him quickly. Cowboys tried without success to capture Red Lodge with lariats. Finally, he was felled by a shot in the abdomen, and the frenzied whites beat and stabbed him into insensibility, leaving him for dead.

Later, an Agency farmer found Red Lodge alive. At Arapahoe, a physician treated the young man for his multiple wounds, and a troop of cavalry arrived at the town to protect Red Lodge and other Indians from maltreatment. A subsequent investigation proved Red Lodge innocent of the crime. In the neighboring town of Watonga, six Indians and four Whites testified at Red Lodge's trial that he was in their town when the alleged assault occurred. Red Lodge was declared innocent by the jury; he eventually recovered from his wounds.[20]

When reservations opened, Indians became minorities in their own lands. Each white occupational group came to consider Indians as a resource to be looted. If possible, Indians tended to live away from white settlers or around small towns. They were sought, however, by farmers and ranchers who wanted to lease unused allotments. Merchants enticed Indians to buy unneeded goods at inflated prices, and real estate jobbers early in the twentieth century sought to buy trust land from unlettered Indians as soon as they were declared competent or were the inheritors of allotments of deceased relatives. Bankers and lawyers found it easy to charge usurious interest rates and foreclose in lenient courts upon Indian property not regulated by trust restrictions. Regardless of how a white man made his living, white settlers found some way to appropriate and use Indian property.

White ranchers and farmers, as inhabitants of the prairies and plains, disrupted the Indian way of life. Whether in Indian, Oklahoma, or Dakota Territory, the range operations of cattlemen raised tensions between Whites and Indians. Texas cattlemen and cowboys, never very respectful of Indians, disdained Indian rights. All too frequently, managers of large cattle corporations dealt with Indian agents, mixed-bloods, and a few amenable Indian leaders to obtain leases or to rent millions of acres of range land for a small fraction of the land's market value. During the 1880s, reservations in Indian and Dakota Territory were filled with cattle herds, while the Indians were restricted to a small portion of their reservation. Promises made that Indians would be taught to herd and raise cattle were soon forgotten. If an Indian possessed a small number of beef cattle, they disappeared when roundups were conducted. Indian ponies could not run free, barbed-wire fences cut up the reservation, and Indian gardens were destroyed by the lessee's stock; Indians, to allay hunger, slaughtered the white man's beef for food. Trail herds of cattle or ponies were driven through Indian camps and cultivated land. If an Indian protested, as happened on occasion, he was beaten and sometimes shot. The legacy of ill will between cattlemen and Indians lasted for several generations in western Indian Territory.

A woman from the Standing Rock Reservation remembers with some bitterness the process by which settlers obtained Indian land. The Bureau of Indian Affairs, Christine Zahn related, sought to help Indian youths who had graduated from Carlisle. " 'You've got land out there,' the Indians were told, 'you're not using it, you don't live out there. So we are going to let homesteaders come in.' So then the white people, homesteaders come in, horse thieves came in, cattle rustlers came in, and in twenty years the Indians were afoot, we were all afoot. We didn't have a horse. That's one of the worst things that ever happened to the Standing Rock Reservation."[21]

Once the cattleman opened one reservation, the pressure to open others increased. At the Cheyenne River Reservation, the Indians in councils refused to lease their lands because they ran their own cattle and they received rations and *per capita* payments from the government. Despite Indian resistance, the cattlemen "wouldn't let them rest. They just kept a'going and they kept a'fighting it anyway. So one day the interpreter . . . said, I'm sorry folks . . . your land is leased." The interpreter was questioned, "who gave them permission?" The agent. "What power did the agent have with this land? This is our land," Louise Hiett insisted, "and w'r using it and a big outfit is going to come in here and they said how many cattle are they going to put in here? About 9,000 cattle. Well then we just [might] as [well] kill all our cattle." The Indians "hollared and kicked," but the Indian agent was bought.[22]

Infrequently, an Indian was not resentful of his white

neighbors. Sam Robertson of the Sisseton-Whapeton group related that the first white farmers in northwestern South Dakota and his people cooperated for some years. The Indian owned wood needed by the white settlers for building and fuel. "The white man and the Indian," Robertson recalled, "got along just like they were brothers.... The white man had plenty to eat but nothing to burn. But the Indian helped the white man and they got help from the white man, meat, pork, anything you wanted."[23]

As time passed, however, Indians reacted against the wealth accumulated by Whites from the use of Indian land. German-Russian immigrants leased Indian land at the Cheyenne River Agency. The land rent was cheap, which allowed the immigrants to buy "big fine cars, tractors and trucks and what not." Louise Hiett believed that the German-Russians did not like Indian people because they lived apart, even building their own church. What the immigrants liked, however, was the money they made from cultivating Indian land.[24] Even the example of the accumulation of property had an unfortunate effect upon Indians. David Frazier, long-time chairman of the Santee Sioux, remembers that troubles arose even between Indians soon after the allotment of the reservation began. The traditional communal practices became fewer as Indians adopted the white attitude, "what's mine is mine. You stay on your side. The idea of the white man, that's what the white man ... brought ... into this country and passed it on to us."[25]

Perceptively, Indians came to understand that among the settler's motivations, economic matters predominated. Little Fish, an old Sioux chief, capsulized the matter very well when he stated: "The white man is a man of business, and has no use for a heart."[26] Unfortunately, the Indians were ill-prepared to cope with either the Long Knives or settlers. Their culture was not prepared to resist continuous campaigns of attrition mounted by the United States army in the 1870s. Neither were the tribes sufficiently prepared to protect their private property from their neighbors who were assisted in their plundering of Indian property by white law. At the turn of the twentieth century, the Plains Indians were nearing the lowest ebb of their existence. Soldiers had contained them on reservations, politicians and philanthropists had seized much reservation land under the Dawes Act, and settlers were preparing to acquire

Indian allotments under the 1902 Dead Indian Land Act and the 1906 Burke Act. Indians asked for justice — few Whites heard their pleas.

Notes

[1] Merrill J. Mattes, *The Great Platte Road: The Covered Wagon Mainline Via Fort Kearny to Fort Laramie*, Nebraska State Historical Society, *Publications*, vol. XXV (Lincoln, Nebr.: Published by the Society, 1969), p. 516.

[2] W. C. Vanderwerth, *Indian Oratory: Famous Speeches by Noted Indian Chiefs* (Norman, Okla.: University of Oklahoma Press, c. 1971), p. 160.

[3] Vanderwerth, *Indian Oratory*, p. 188-189.

[4] Vanderwerth, *Indian Oratory*, p. 126.

[5] Robert M. Utley, *Frontiersmen in Blue: The United States Army and the Indian, 1848-1865* (New York: Macmillan Pub. Co., Inc., c. 1967), p. 113-114.

[6] Utley, *Frontiersmen in Blue*, p. 108.

[7] Utley, *Frontiersmen in Blue*, p. 115-119.

[8] Utley, *Frontiersmen in Blue*, p. 120-125.

[9] Utley, *Frontiersmen in Blue*, p. 128-141.

[10] Vanderwerth, *Indian Oratory*, p.134-135.

[11] Vanderwerth, *Indian Oratory*, p. 142.

[12] Robert M. Utley, *Frontier Regulars: The United States Army and the Indians, 1886-1891* (New York: Macmillan Pub. Co., Inc., c. 1973), p. 99.

[13] Utley, *Frontier Regulars*, p. 108, fn. 17.

[14] Utley, *Frontier Regulars*, p. 135-136.

[15] Vamderwerth, *Indian Oratory*, p. 189.

[16] George Armstrong Custer, *My Life on the Plains* (Norman, Okla.: University of Oklahoma Press, c. 1962), p. 13.

[17] *Ex parte Crow Dog*, 109 U.S. 556 (1883).

[18] Charles Alexander Eastman (Ohiyesa), *The Soul of the Indian: An Interpretation* (Boston and New York: Houghton-Mifflin Company, c. 1911), p. 110-113.

[19] James McLaughlin, *My Friend the Indian* (Boston and New York: Houghton Mifflin Company, 1910), p. 303-306.

[20] A. E. Woodson to Richard Davis, June 11, 12, 1895; Woodson to T. S. Shahan, June 12, 1895; Woodson to Captain J. C. Mackey, June 17, 1895; Mackey to Woodson, June 16, 1895; Woodson to Commissioner of Indian Affairs, June 24, 1895; Woodson to *Wichita Eagle* and *Kansas City Times*, June 25, 1895; Woodson to Little Man and Chief White Horse and the Indians of the Cantonment District, June 26, 1895; Cheyenne and Arapaho Agency Letterbooks, Indian Archives, Oklahoma Historical Society, Oklahoma City, Okla., vol. 50: pp. 134-135, 143-145, 158-159, 213-215, 257, 258, 259-262, 311-317, 318-320, 333-336.

[21] Interview of Robert and Christine Zahn, MS. 359, p. 14, Institute of Indian Studies, University of South Dakota, Vermillion, South Dakota.

[22] Interview of Louise Hiett, MS. 694, p. 5, Institute of Indian Studies, USD.

[23] Interview of Sam Robertson, MS. 432, pp. 6, 18, Institute of Indian Studies, USD.

[24] Interview of Louise Hiett, MS. 694, p. 45, Institute of Indian Studies, USD.

[25] Interview of David Frazier, MS. 769, pp. 15-16, Institute of Indian Studies, USD.

[26] Charles A. Eastman, *From the Deep Woods of Civilization: Chapters in the Autobiography of an Indian* (Boston: Little, Brown, and Company, 1916), p. 161.

Dale Crawford '75

The Arrival of Emigrants & Soldiers: Curiosity, Contempt, Confusion & Conflict

Robert L. Munkres, Muskingum College

During the middle decade of the last century, large numbers (by nineteenth century standards) of Anglo-Americans moved across the High Plains toward the mountains and beyond in search of land and gold. By the end of the seventh decade of the century, this flow of humanity had reversed itself and, still searching for gold and land, returned to the High Plains to claim it for their own. In the course of this movement, Whites came increasingly into contact with the various tribes of American Indians native to the region. The varying white reactions to the indigenous population may be summarized under four broad headings: curiosity, contempt (for many things Indian, conceit about most things white), confusion, and conflict. Clearly, these four "c's" are not equally apt descriptions for all groups at all times. At least two general warnings ought to be noted in conjunction with the use of such categories.

First, the creation of categories and the ordering of data through the use of such categories is a prerequisite to the rational consideration of any matter. Categories thus created, however, all too easily are themselves reduced to simplistic stereotypes and through the use of these, perceptive evaluation is rendered difficult, if not impossible. Further, there is always the danger that categories created as intellectual tools may come to be accepted as reality itself.

Secondly, it must be remembered that not only were a number of different Indian tribes involved, but that a nearly equivalent variety marked the white population which moved west. Thus, we must attempt to define some of those attitudes about Indians common to most emigrants and settlers, yet take care to note that even common attitudes and values may differ substantially in application to specific situations by specific individuals. Although its complete validity may be questionable, it is always well to remember the caveat of Justice Holmes to the effect that no generalization is worth a damn (including, one supposes, this one!)[1]

With this in mind, white reactions to American Indians may nonetheless be summarized. Among the Oregon pilgrims and California gold rushers, curiosity and contempt (conceit), in various mixtures, tended to dominate. As settlement increased, with an attendant expansion of governmental authority, confusion all too frequently replaced curiosity, and conflict — the fourth horseman of this intellectual apocalypse — permeated the entire relationship.

Curiosity

One of the earliest points of Indian-White contact in large numbers was the annual rendezvous of the fur trade era. Not surprisingly, the Indians in attendance at these "trade fairs" were usually viewed in quite a favorable light. John Ball (1832) and William Marshall Anderson (1834) both were impressed by the Nez Perce and Flathead Indians. The former described them as "decent and interesting" in terms of personal appearance and "decidedly honest and friendly";[2] the latter were described as being "proverbial for their honesty and love for truth."[3]

The Shoshonis, frequently present at rendezvous, consistently maintained a reputation of friendliness toward Whites, not infrequently trading horses, dressed skins, and other items as they did with William Newby in 1843 near the Bear River.[4] Three years later, Edwin Bryant reacted most favorably upon encountering Shoshoni warriors: "Many of the men we saw were finely formed for strength and agility, with countenances expressive of courage and humanity. They evinced fine horsemanship and skillful use of the bow and arrow, their principal weapon in hunting and war."[5] These and subsequent descriptions, whether positive or negative, with some frequency convey an impression that their authors viewed the indigenous inhabitants of the region as simply part of "The Wild Life of the Great Plains and Mountains."

In view of the reputation they subsequently acquired, it is interesting to note that during the years of greatest travel on the Oregon-California Trail, the Dakota were rather highly regarded by emigrants. Sioux were normally encountered, if at all, in the North Platte Valley. At Ash Hollow, Robert Chalmers (1850) described some Indian visitors as "very friendly";[6] almost a year later in the same general area, Mrs. E. A. Hadley (1851) wrote that "the tribe of Soos [sic] ... are kind and hospitable and are the most polite and cleanest tribe on the road. They are whiter, to, than any that we have seen. They are well dressed and made a fine appearance."[7] Farther up the valley, near Chimney Rock and Scotts Bluff, other emigrants described parties of Sioux as "quite intelegent [sic]"[8] and as "very friendly and sociable, with free and open countenances, well dressed ... in blue strouding and scarlet cloth ... their faces were not disfigured with paint like most of those immediately on our frontiers."[9] During these earlier years, Sioux actions sometimes startled pilgrims, as did the Oglala leader who, near the fork of the Platte, offered Asahel Munger's party (1839) "a guard to watch our horses if we wanted to keep the Indians from stealing them."[10]

Females of the Plains tribes were considered by many to be very attractive. One diarist described Crow women as "stately and full of grace ... daughter[s] of the wilderness, dressed in a closely fitting buckskin robe, trimmed with collar in red, set with shining white dog's teeth...."[11] Forty years after Sacajawea had impressed Lewis and Clark, Edwin Bryant (1846) "noticed a very beautiful young female, the daughter of one of the chiefs of the party, who sat upon her horse with the ease and grace almost of a fairy.... It will be a long time before I forget the cheerful and attractive countenance, graceful figure, and vivacity of feature and language of this untutored child of nature."[12] Some three weeks earlier, Mr. Bryant had waxed equally eloquent over the appearance of Sioux women observed at Fort Laramie. "Many of these women," he wrote, "for regularity of features and symmetry of figure, would bear off the palm of beauty from some of our most celebrated belles. A portion of the Sioux women are decidedly beautiful.... The student of sculpture, when he has acquired his trade at Rome or Florence, should erect his studio among the Sioux for his models."[13] Such opinions as these were, of course, by no means universally held. George Keller (1850) spoke for who knows how many when he flatly stated, "I have never seen a single specimen" of beauty among Indian women.[14] Asa Brown in the same year probably represented the attitude of a good many white men when he observed that while "many of the females [are] decidedly good looking," they would not be acceptable in white society, or, as he put it, "squaws who appear lovely in a wigwam lose most of their attractions when transferred to a parlor."[15]

Although, as will be noted later, they were very poorly regarded by most emigrants, on occasion kind words were written even about the Pawnees. Even though he recognized that "they are frequently very troublesome to the Santa Fe Traders in stealing their horses and mules," Reverend Pearson Barton Reading (1843) described Pawnees on the Blue River as being "different from other Indians in one respect, they do not beg. They bear the character of being a proud and honorable nation."[16] Some seven years later, near the ford of the South Platte, Charles Ferguson (1850) had a more pragmatic reason for being impressed "with a small band of Pawnees ... [who] were friendly and of great service to us" because "They warned us to beware of the Sioux, as they were very mean and would lie and steal; ... they ... told us the truth ... for a bigger set of thieves no one ever fell in with."[17]

It is apparent that much white contact with Indians on the trail was friendly. In addition to the physical descriptions already noted, emigrants described in some detail the activities in Indian camps as well as their method of moving and setting up a village. George Keller's party (1850), in fact, threw away many of their guns at Ash Hollow because they were certain no problems with Indians would occur.[18] It should further be noted that quite a few wagon trains, while crossing the high plains, encountered virtually no Indians except at forts and trading posts.[19] Of those who did record meetings with Indians, however, the types of descriptions noted above appeared in only a minority of the journals. In fact, some of those who described contact with certain Indians in quite positive terms, reacted most unfavorably to others. In many such cases, the difference in reaction was as much the result of what had happened to the writer during the interval between descriptions as it was to significant differences between the Indians involved. Upon arriving at the Comanche Agency in Texas in 1857, Matthew Leeper described the "residents" as being "naturally intellectual ...

[with] a high sense of propriety in dress and becoming deport-
ment ... [who] are content and happy, and satisfied to live a
quiet and settled life."[20] In 1859, Leeper was attacked and
nearly killed by an Indian. His annual report for the following
year contained the following: "All Indians with whom I am acquainted are an improvident people, they have no care for the
future; when they have plenty, they will eat most inordinately,
revel over it, sing, dance, and sleep until it is gone, and then
they will complain for the want of more supplies."[21]

Contempt (Conceit)

The Sioux, who, as we have seen, were very favorably
described by a number of emigrants, also had their fair share of
detractors. One of their own agents who later married (then
abandoned) a Sioux woman, called them "uneducated &
childlike."[22]

The year 1864 was a dangerous one for Whites on the
trail. In June of that year, George Forman, speaking for a great
many emigrants before and after him, called "a large number of
Painted Sioux ... very courageous but treacherous, blood-
thirsty and cruel."[23] The Sioux, in common with all the other
tribes encountered, according to Charles Ferguson (1850), "had
not been misrepresented touching their pilfering qualities — in
fact, they would rob."[24] One young man attempted to steal some
pancakes from a tin plate but succeeded only in knocking them
to the ground. When he bent over to pick them up, Ferguson
decked him with a frying pan, splashing hot grease on the Indian's head and face in the process. The other Sioux in the
camp, instead of seeking vengeance, "seemed to enjoy the joke,
for they laughed at him, and he appeared to be ashamed."[25]
Reactions such as this to the contrary notwithstanding, many
Whites during the 1860s felt the Sioux were, for the most part,
unfeeling. The commanding officer at Fort Laramie said as
much when he described the burial of Spotted Tail's daughter at
the fort; he noted that the impressive ceremony "produced a
marked effect upon all the Indians present, and satisfied some
who had never before seemed to believe it, that an Indian had a
human heart to work on, and was not a wild animal."[26]

Men of the various Dakota bands were not the only native
inhabitants to enjoy a very mixed reputation among Whites;
they were, in this respect, effectively matched by Crow

warriors. As early as 1834, they were referred to as "the most expert and incorrigible rogues on the face of the earth,"[27] a description heartily seconded by most mountain men and emigrants. The Crow reputation, however, did differ from that of most Plains tribes in two ways. First, according to William Chandless (1855), "Crows never kill a white man, and if they find him in want will give him food, but they will strip him of all superfluities if they can. . . ."[28] Secondly, the Crows on occasion accomplished the latter with a style that bordered on rough and ready humor. One example must suffice. An enlisted man deserted at Fort Laramie, stole the colonel's horse, and headed for the gold fields of California. Several days later, he returned to the fort, naked except for a buffalo robe, riding a horse that clearly had seen better days. About a hundred miles west of Fort Laramie, it seems the soldier had encountered a band of Crows who, in exchange for his clothes, horse, and equipment, gave him a buffalo robe and a broken down nag and told him to return to the fort. The emigrant who related this incident further noted: "This with the Crows is not deemed robbing or stealing, but a pure business transaction, not unlike, though in a humbler degree, a modern Wall Street operation, though in the latter instance, the winning party rarely contributes even a blanket to cover the nakedness of the party fleeced."[29] This is not to imply that pilgrims normally looked upon Crows as resident "good humor" men. To the contrary, most agreed with the attitude of John Kearns (1852): "they look crowish enough to eat us if they dared."[30]

During the years of heavy travel on the road west, it was generally true that those tribes encountered during the first weeks on the trail were almost universally viewed with distaste. Perhaps most travelers did not (or could not) distinguish between and among the tribes involved, contenting themselves with such observations as "These Indians are decidedly a dissipated and debased people, having acquired all the vices and none of the virtues of the whites."[31] The following illustrates those attitudes which were expressed about some of the specific tribes in eastern Kansas and Nebraska. Omaha: "the first tribe we pass through, they are the most filthy thevist [sic] set and are mostly naked."[32] Potowatami: "They are a filthy tribe and barbarois [sic]. . . ."[33] Iowa and Sac: "nations who live together. Are generally a good looking race, large, robust, have however [a] sneaking physiognomy."[34] Kansas: "Find them to be miserable wretches begging for food and stealing all they can lay their hands on."[35] Osage: "they were very sociable but looked like devils."[36]

Other tribes all along the trail also incurred the descriptive wrath of white travelers. The roots of their antipathy went deep! In February of 1827, one subsequently recurring theme in Anglo-American thought was expressed by the British leader of fur-trapping brigades, Peter Skene Ogden: "We all know Indians are treacherous, blood-thirsty. The sooner the exterminating system be introduced among them the better."[37] The first agent for the Upper Platte and Arkansas Agency was among those who wove two more threads into the intellectual pattern of white thought about Indians. In 1847, Thomas Fitzpatrick, while praising the government for attempting "to do all it can for them," described the Plains Indians as "a doomed race ... [who] must fulfill their destiny."[38] Not quite four months later, in opposing the use by the military of Indian "irregulars," he generalized that "their well known faithlessness and treachery and between whom no difference exists in regard to villany [sic] ought to be forever a bar against such proceedings."[39]

One final general theme should be noted. In support of a bill to construct military roads along the western frontier, Congressman Richard M. Johnson of Kentucky submitted a report to the House on March 3, 1836. In this report, Johnson stated that (1) savage Indians pose a substantial threat to outlying settlements; (2) if Indians understood what would happen to them because of their actions, they would not be hostile; and (3) Indians do not draw such logical conclusions because "they are savages, uncivilized and unenlightened — creatures of passion and momentary impulse."[40]

In some instances, diarists verbally attacked Indians by comparing them with other racial and/or ethnic groups which were then held to be inferior to Whites. Enoch Conyers (1852) and John Ball (1832) each provide an example. Conyers decried the presence of Pawnee Indians in camp because "the Italian Gypsy cannot beat them in begging."[41] Mr. Ball, on September 17, noted, "the Indians were kind and friendly ... but they could not forgo the attempt to steal our horses ... any more than a negro can leave a hen roost alone."[42] It should also be noted that not all emigrants who thought poorly of Indians contented themselves with recording derogatory descriptions.

69

"Lots of Indians come to camp to beg and steal," wrote E. S. Mc-Comas (1862), "I burned one's back with my sun glass and gave another bread with cyyan [sic] pepper. They stopped."[43]

The subject of negative reactions to Indians cannot be left without at least a mention of one more tribe. Among most emigrants, there was little question that the Pawnees, year in and year out, won the prize for being the least like Rousseau's "noble savage." Jason Lee (1834) thought them to be "generally . . . a treacherous tribe";[44] to Edwin Bryant (1846), they were "reported to be vicious savages, and skillful and daring thieves."[45] While J. Quinn Thornton (1846) thought Pawnees "looked much better than either the Kansas or the Shawnee Indians," he nonetheless described them as "insolent and pertinacious in their alternative absolute demands, and begging solicitations for food."[46] Finally, William Johnston (1849) may well have summed up emigrant reaction to Pawnees when he observed that "they have acquired the reputation honestly — the only thing perhaps ever obtained by them in that mode — of being a cunning, cut-throat race of villains, with an endless propensity for stealing."[47] Mrs. Velina Williams (1853) agreed that Pawnees would steal; one night they "killed four oxen and badly wounded the fifth, belonging to some emigrants."[48] She went on, however, to express an opinion a bit unusual among emigrants: "They [emigrants] no doubt gave the Indians some cause for committing the outrage."[49]

Clearly the attitudes of many, and probably most, Whites manifested varying degrees of contempt for most things Indian; it appears that an equally large number were morally certain, to the point of conceit, of the superiority of white values. Sometimes the feeling of superiority, while present, was expressed almost as an afterthought. C. W. Smith, for example, coming through Ash Hollow in May of 1850, described a band of Sioux as "quite friendly"; he then noted that "they look quite intelligent for Indians and superior to what I had expected to see".[50] The following year, D. D. Mitchell, commenting on the Fort Laramie Treaty of 1851, said that the agreement was an attempt to "solve the great problem — whether or not an Indian can be made a civilized man."[51]

Indian evidence in disputes was definitely suspect. Thomas Twiss, Upper Platte Agent, thought his communications were being tampered with by other Whites. He did not propose to do anything but report the matter to his superior because "I have only the evidence of Indians that my Express men have been tampered with. . . ."[52] When subsequent evidence cleared Indians of accusations made against them, belief of guilt frequently remained. William Bent sent word to Lt. Henry Heth that a man supposedly killed by Cheyennes had been done away with by one of his own companions. Upon receipt of this information, Lt. Heth wrote, "Although I still think the Chyannes [sic] committed the murder . . . [now] there was a shadow of a doubt in my mind, which of course had to be given to the cause of humanity. . . ."[53]

In some instances, of course, feelings of white superiority were so clearly, even bluntly, stated as to require no interpretation at all. Two examples, the first positive, the second negative, will suffice.

> I feel it unnecessary to enumerate the causes, which present themselves intuitively to the white man, of which the genius of his race is the final one, for settling these Indians upon reservations, and teaching them the rudiments of civilization. This course recommends itself to the Anglo-American, to the end that his imperial energies and capacities should not be circumscribed, save by the natural boundaries of the earth.[54]

> It [Indian courage] is a hard and stoical insensibility, unworthy of being ranked among the virtues of civilization. Instead of being a patriotic courage, which causes us to respect the unhappy captive, it is an unfeeling savage, and brutal insensibility; to confound which with true heroism, would be to break down the distinctions between virtue and vice, and to confound all in chaotic confusion.

> Indians are generally cowards; and they will seldom fight without a decided advantage in numbers, weapons, or position. In short, the virtues usually attributed to them are figments of the brain, and have no existence in fact. Virtue is a plant which does not grow in the coldness and darkness of barbarism, but in the genial warmth and benign light of civilization and Christianity.[55]

Confusion

As a key element in Indian-White relations, confusion sprang from a number of sources. Among the principal sources, one might list ignorance, prejudice (already described to some extent), and selective perception resulting in gross misinterpretations.

Even a cursory examination of the history of Indian-White relations quickly reveals the extensive lack of information and knowledge which existed. Indians, for instance, had no realistic notion as to how many Whites there were, let alone the likely long-term effect of such numbers. In 1843, more than half a decade before the numbers of Whites moving west reached really substantial levels, at least some Indians were convinced that there could be very few left in the east![56] White sophistication about things Indian, unfortunately, was at no higher a level. Thomas Fitzpatrick was of the opinion, for example, that the tribes of the Upper Platte and Arkansas "have no fixed laws, or anything like permanent institutions by which to regulate" their internal affairs and relations with other tribes.[57] He argued that intertribal warfare was, in large part, the result of the uncertainty resulting from this procedural vacuum.[58]

Some ten months later, Fitzpatrick recognized the importance of army officers being "well acquainted with Indian character, habits, custom, and above all, their mode of warfare."[59] He strongly urged that "great care be taken in the selection of officers to take command of their battalion," because it was the lack "of this knowledge that has been the cause for the past few years of the total failure of all the expeditions made against the Indians. . . ."[60] The extent to which his advice was effectively taken is illustrated by the 1865 report of Major General Alexander McCook. In that report, the general stated that one of the major causes of "Indian troubles upon the Plains" was "the inexperience and almost total ignorance of Volunteer officers of Indian character. . . ."[61]

A definition of warfare was frequently the subject of differing interpretations by Indians and by Whites. Fighting, for Indians, was normally undertaken for individual prestige, not as an instrument of group policy. If the purpose of warfare differed, so also did the manner in which it was carried out. As the Earl of Dunraven pointed out, "They [Indians] look upon our bravery as the height of folly, and find us lacking entirely in those great qualities they so much admire. . . . Their mode of carrying on war is quite dissimilar to ours, and they do not . . . highly esteem a man who is ready at all times to sacrifice his life for the cause."[62] It would, apparently, have been hard to explain to "savages" Grant's brilliant victory in the Wilderness! It was equally difficult for Whites to appreciate what a warrior was being required to give up when a treaty was signed under the terms of which horse stealing was outlawed.

Within the context of Plains Indian culture, combat brought a type of prestige that could be acquired in no other way. Yet, the economic gain and related social prestige that were earned by raiding and by counting coups was always thought of by Whites as something to be eliminated rather than replaced. In their own society, however, reward systems that were only thinly disguised surrogates for warfare had long since been accepted. Perhaps the major reason such white practices were not readily transferable to Indian society derived from the fact that individual competition among the Indians was primarily directed toward other groups (tribes); in Anglo-American society, on the other hand, a premium was placed on competing directly against other members of your own group. In any event, white policy-makers took as evidence of Indian faithlessness, savagery, etc. the failure of treaties to eliminate in short order their decades-old intertribal warfare.[63]

It was, however, in the area of treaty negotiations that confusion had a field day (unbeknownst, though, to the participants). In the first place, the usage of the term "Great White Father" by Whites was always heavily laced with a near monarchical or royalist emphasis on inherent authority and a demand for almost unquestioning obedience. Such an approach is at least theoretically valid as between an absolute ruler and his subjects — but as an approach to negotiation between equals, it leaves something to be desired![64]

The very assumption that treaty negotiations were an appropriate vehicle for dealing with Indian affairs was itself productive of at least one illogical (and unfulfilled) behavioral expectation. Indian tribes were frequently referred to as "nations." The term is correctly used insofar as the Indians concerned collectively considered themselves a "people" (although it must be noted, individual loyalty seemed to be centered on the band or tribe rather than the entire "nation"). Whites, however, almost uniformly equated "nations" with "states" because of their own western European intellectual heritage. They thus expected Indian "nations" to behave politically like sovereign "states"; treaties, after all, are only negotiated between states.[65] It is doubtful that the words "sovereign state" could even be translated into an Indian language in any meaningful way. Certainly Plains Indians' socio-political systems had no institutions or practices which corresponded to such a definition.

Most treaties between the United States Government and Indian tribes called for the payment of stipulated amounts of annuity goods to the tribes for a specified period of time. In return for such payments, the Indian signatories first granted rights of passage, and later ceded land itself to the government, as well as promising not to "molest" white travelers and/or settlers. Some treaties also contained promises to refrain from intertribal warfare.

Assuming that the amount paid in annuity goods was fair (and this is an entire area of controversy in itself), the misinterpretation and confusion implicit in the treaty-making process may be highlighted with four questions. First, is it reasonable to assume that the tribes knew what they were giving up? Can one realistically believe that the technical language of treaties (and the amendments sometimes subsequently added) were truly comprehensible to the Indians involved? Or is it, perhaps, more accurate to believe that Whites merely assumed Indian understanding of English legal terminology? Second, were the tribes aided or hindered in making such arrangements subsequent to the treaty as might be necessary for their own continued survival? Third (as an outgrowth of the second question), once having concluded an agreement with a tribe (as an independent negotiating body), was the major thrust of federal policy thereafter to work through the tribal structure or to break it down, with the goal of replacing it with political leadership more amenable to white direction and with a political structure more consistent with white expectations? Fourth, was the time span of treaties realistic in view of the tremendous cultural change being contemplated? Virtually no one in authority seriously considered the possibility that such change might be legitimately undesirable from the Indians' point of view and even unattainable for all practical purposes. Let us examine several points in regard to each of these questions.

The first question immediately raises the general issue of territory and land. One does not have to probe very deeply into the two cultures with which we are concerned to learn that very substantial differences existed in terms both of land ownership and of land use. More will be said later on this topic. Let it here suffice simply to note that such concepts of ownership of real estate as existed in Plains Indian culture bore very little, if any, resemblance to the legal and constitutional attributes of property in the American political system. So far as land use was concerned, although several tribes did do some farming, Indians were far more prone than Whites to live off the natural produce of the land rather than to subsist on what they conceivably could create out of it. Whites, on the other hand, were heavily agrarian in orientation; they thus viewed the land essentially as a resource to be used by individual owners for their own benefit. Indian concepts of land use did not uniformly preclude different individuals from using the same land; in contrast, white concepts tended very much in this direction.[66]

Indian and white understanding of each other's positions during treaty negotiations depended in part on the ability to communicate either in a common language or through an interpreter. Contrary to the idea spawned by movies, "the 'sign language' that [is] common to all the wild tribes of the west, while it might answer the purposes of barter could not be relied upon in matters of so much importance and delicacy."[67] Furthermore, the trustworthiness of interpreters was suspect in many quarters. Ashton White informed the Secretary of the Interior that he had very little confidence in any interpreter; he added "that no consultation is held with Indians, unless there are two or more persons present to deny or affirm the correctness of the Interpreter. Where it requires three men to watch one, the honesty and fidelity of either may be doubted."[68] Thomas Fitzpatrick was even less kind; according to "Broken Hand," "the most ignorant and weakminded are those who most readily acquire knowledge of the Indian tongue orally. From this cause, it is a very difficult matter to arrive at anything like correctness...."[69] As noted earlier in connection with the concept of sovereignty, some concepts from one culture may simply have no counterpart in another; it is very difficult to explain the phenomenon of light to one who was born blind.

The answer to the second question can be simply stated. Indians who adopted white ways were not overtly hindered; those who attempted to maintain the old ways were. In neither case were Indians "aided" in any substantive sense, but all bore certain burdens because of their racial origin: (1) A varying number of Whites — but always some — held to the view that most Indians were dishonest and untrustworthy. Some opinions which support this assertion have already been cited. Bvt.

Major Johnson of the 6th Infantry furnishes still another. Referring to an apparent treaty violation by Comanches, Major Johnson wrote, "It seems to show what little reliance can be placed in the faith of these people and how slightly they regard the obligations of treaties...."[70] (2) Treaty violations by individual Indians or by small bands usually resulted in demands and/or action aginst the entire tribe. In addressing the problem of alleged violations of the Fort Laramie Treaty of 1868 by Oglala warriors, Felix Brunot and Robert Campbell made a very salient, but frequently disregarded, point when they observed that "it would be unreasonable to expect that Red Cloud can maintain among his savage followers a degree of virtue, and exemption from criminality, more absolute than the Authorities are able to secure in our most enlightened communities."[71] (3) Not all Whites by any means wanted peace between Whites and Indians, because war was more profitable. As Superintendent of Indian Affairs E. B. Taylor put it in 1866, "What I most fear is, that parties interested in the fitting out and subsistence of armies, will continue their efforts to produce ... a war until they will prove successful."[72] One year earlier, Senator James Doolittle of Wisconsin wrote his wife:

> So many people live by having wars go on among Indians. So many white men rob and steal and charge it upon the Indians. So many bad Indians whom their chiefs cannot control will steal and depredate. So many white men on the frontier hunt Indians as they hunt wild beasts, and so many blundering lieutenants in the army by some imprudent act will plunge at once into an Indian war, that we almost despair of having peace till the Indians are exterminated.[73]

Some Whites, of course, had always attempted to saddle Indians with responsibility for their own criminal acts. In 1850, Robert Chalmers' "company ... lost 5 horses and 14 oxen, which were stolen by Indians or Whites for they are worse than Indians. They steal here and take them back and sell again to emigrants."[74] Three years later, Henry Allyn learned that "the body of the man ... that was shot at the ferry, is found.... It was a white man with an Indian blanket around him, endeavoring to steal on Indian credit. Judgment overtook him suddenly."[75]

Regarding question number three — it is clear that the goverment never accepted the traditional tribal structure as a suitable vehicle through which Indian policy could be implemented. Felix Brunot put it quite clearly when he suggested

that Indians should "be made to understand that for the commission of any offense ... [they] would be tried and punished,
and coupling this with the abolishment of the tribal relation ...
would ... do more to civilize them than anything else. Here we
recognize the chiefs and sanction the barbarous tribal relation."[76] Chiefs and Head Men were sometimes treated as if they
were simply extensions of the Executive Branch. In commenting upon General Harney's agreement with the Sioux at Fort
Pierre, the Secretary of War stated that "the Chiefs and
Soldiers of each Band being once recognized are liable to
removal only on application to the President. By this means the
authority of the Executive will be represented and maintained
by the Tribal Chiefs ... with the aid of the police or
'soldiers'...."[77] A decade later, General Sully, however, complained that everyone was creating "chiefs, Military Comman-
ders, Superintendents of Indian Affairs, Indian Commissioners,
even Indian Agents," with the result "that Indian Chiefs, like
Privates in the Army, are becoming so common, they are not
properly respected."[78] It is small wonder that one of the agents
for the Upper Platte observed that "the policy of dividing to con-
quer is as proper in diplomacy as on the battlefield."[79]

Finally, to the last question, which concerns the time span
encompassed by many treaties. Two of those most directly
responsible for the Fort Laramie Treaty of 1851, Thomas
Fitzpatrick and D. D. Mitchell, were both convinced that time
was necessary, "because such a change in the habits and
customs of such people must be brought by slow, gradual, and
judicious action."[80] This statement clearly assumes that the
worth of a treaty was to be measured not by the length of time it
was to be in effect, but rather by the extent to which its operation contributed to the complete cultural conversion of the
tribes involved. During the nineteenth century, it occurred to
very few Whites that a policy of cultural conversion might well
be impractical and perhaps unethical.

The three principal policy weapons in the battle against
Indian culture were education, farming, and Christianity. The
first would cause Indian children to "acquire new habits, new
ideas, new modes of life; the old Indians would die off, and carry
with them all the latent longings for murdering and robbing ...";[81] thus, "this Evil will pass away with the present
generation, when the mind and habits of the young can be
moulded to usefulness."[82]

Within the context of Indian affairs, "usefulness" normally translated "farming." The agrarian myth was deeply imbedded in the Anglo-American mind. In 1874, for example, the Commissioner of Indian Affairs divided the Indian population into three groups: (1) the wild ones, (2) those "convinced of the necessity of labor . . . and with more or less readiness [to] accept . . . direction and assistance," and (3) "Indians who have come into possession of allotted land and other property in stock and implements belonging to a landed estate."[83] There is no question as to which of these three groups was thought to be the most civilized. Attachment to a small acreage would, it was thought, imbue Indians with those values cherished by all Americans, or, as Senator Pendleton put it, "this trinity upon which all civilization depends — family, and home, and property."[84] Senator Dawes was less theological; property would eliminate the fatal flaw in traditional Indian society. What was the flaw? "There is no selfishness, which is at the bottom of civilization."[85]

For many Whites, there was some confusion as to whether the purpose of introducing Christianity among the Indians was to convert or simply to pacify, if indeed such a distinction was drawn. Fitzpatrick commented that, for some reason, the Indians living where Whites wanted to settle seemed to need "civilizing" more than did their brethren in more remote parts of the country; at least, missionaries seemed to go in greater numbers to areas of potential white settlement as opposed to remote Indian villages.[86] One cattleman spoke for a great many non-missionary Whites when he suggested that "civilization must come before Christianity — teach them to be peaceable citizens first, and Christians afterwards."[87]

Christianity had not, in the view of many, been too successful either in converting or in pacifying enough Indians. According to an old miner from northern Idaho, however, another product of the white man's genius had been quite adequate for the task: "What a miracle rum has wrought. What Christianity and civilization could not accomplish in decades, liquor has accomplished in a few short months."[88]

Conflict

The remaining facet of Indian-White contact — conflict — is not a surprising result of cultural confrontation. Representatives of one culture not infrequently adopt elimination of competing cultures as a step required for their own survival. Such a policy always carries with it the threat, implicit or explicit, of resort to force when deemed necessary. Before we examine the extent to which this idea manifested itself in Anglo-American thought, two other general factors which contributed quite directly to conflict should be noted. First, the incredible and continuing hassle which permeated relations between and among Indian agents, traders, military authorities, and various "Peace Commission" negotiators certainly militated against successful policy execution, regardless of the particular policy involved. Second, the manner in which white "rules" were applied to Indians frequently did little to create an expectation of fair treatment on the part of the latter.

One commander of the Department of the West, for instance, suggested "that in all cases of wrong committed by an Indian, his tribe should be deprived of annuities and presents until reparations be made. . . ."[89] It does not appear that anyone ever contemplated the same approach in cases of white violations of treaty provisions. In regard to the matter of reparations and/or "punishment," an interesting situation prevailed. Indians deemed guilty of felonious conduct were frequently punished on the basis of white standards; Whites who were similarly guilty were usually assessed penalties (if at all) on the basis of Indian standards. For example, Indians accused of stealing or attacking Whites might well be incarcerated; Whites charged with attacking Indians might be required to pay for an Indian's death with presents of horses.[90] Within the context of their own legal systems, Indians viewed incarceration as being extremely harsh punishment, while the requirement of the payment of horses hardly constituted a significant deterrent to Whites.

The proposed use of force for purposes of chastisement and of pacification was always a part of white thinking in regard to Indians. In the early part of the century, Peter Ogden stated flatly that "Indians in general give us no credit for humanity, but attribute our not revenging murders to cowardice. . . . I am of the opinion if on first discovery of a strange tribe a dozen of them were shot, it would be the means of preserving many lives."[91] Twenty-one years later, Thomas Fitzpatrick made essentially the same point in somewhat less forcible language, noting that "Indians are not at all aware of our capacity or power to chastise them & never will believe it until they have ... [had] a severe chastisement — that once done ... would be the means of putting a stop to the frequent robberies and murders in that country."[92]

"Every emigrant, before leaving for California in '49-'50, equipped himself with some kind of a gun, with which to protect himself from Indians, as well as to shoot wild game."[93] Thus wrote one emigrant of 1850, and there was some reason for such action. Two weeks before the statement above was written, John McGlashen "passed ... some Indians. They looked at us as invaders of their country, and seemed determined to give us no information."[94]

Armed intruders viewed as invaders are prime ingredients for an explosive mixture, and as the numbers involved steadily increased, so did the potentiality for conflict. In the years immediately before the Civil War, the Superintendent of the Southern Indian Superintendency wrote, "... necessity is the supreme law of nations. All along the Indian border the country is now populous, and the railroad will soon reach their frontier. Necessity will soon compel the incorporation of their country into the Union, and before its stern requisitions every other consideration will give way, and even wrong find, as it ever does, in necessity its apology."[95]

In the north, in 1857, Lt. Warren was equally certain in his assessment that "there are ... many inevitable causes at work to produce a war with the Dakota before many years.... They will not, I think, permit the occupation of these hills [Black Hills] without offering a determined resistance."[96]

After the conclusion of hostilities in the Civil War, ever larger numbers of Whites moved west, with a corresponding increase of tension and potential conflict. In 1865, General McCook summarized the alternatives available to the government in dealing with the Indians of the High Plains and mountains. In his view, the government could (1) abandon to the Indians all territory west of Kansas and east of California and Nevada, (2) put the Indians "upon good Reservations" and station troops "in their midst to compel them to live there," and (3) apply "the cruel war of extermination."[97] The first alternative "cannot be carried out," and the third "is so cruel and inhumane that the idea of it cannot be entertained."[98] In the General's view, that left reservations, policed by troops. Such a policy, while obviously superior to the third alternative, nonetheless carried with it a high probability of conflict — certainly with Indians and very possibly with some Whites.

Two telegrams from General Sherman in May of 1870 illustrate the army's problem and response. On May 12, addressing the proposed trip of Red Cloud to Washington, Sherman informed General Augur, "If no Indian Agent comes you may send an officer along. They could strike the road at Sanders or even further west and come through Cheyenne in the cars without stopping. If you apprehend violance at Cheyenne, you should take precaution to protect them, for it would be an infamous outrage if Indians in the custody of their Agents should be molested."[99] Almost a week later, he sent a message to General Sheridan in Helena. Some railroad personnel on Big Sandy had been murdered, and citizen volunteers were being organized for pursuit of the killers, who "should be pursued to the death."[100] "In a recent case," Sherman pointed out, "the Indians on being captured turned out to be white men in disguise. Such men are as bad if not worse than Indians and are not entitled to mercy."[101] While it was doubtful that "any of Red Cloud's Sioux can be so far south as Sandy . . . if so, not one should be spared if found in possession of the stolen stock."[102]

As Whites claimed more and more of the land, the likelihood of open conflict was readily perceived by some of the military. Commenting on the "fertility and freshness, . . . [the] variety of resource, and delightful climate" of the Black Hills, Captain William Ludlow of Custer's 1874 expedition to that area predicted that it "will eventually . . . [be] the home of a thronging population."[103] For such a development as "this, however, the final solution of the Indian question is an indispensable preliminary. . . . The Indians have no country father west to which they can migrate."[104]

If the military was the instrument of conflict, numerous civilian voices in the west called for its wide-scale use. The editor of the *Cheyenne Leader* on April 3, 1868, called for peace with the Indians only after "the roving destroyers are whipped into subjection . . . and humbly beg for life and mercy on any terms which shall be dictated by the invincible whites."[105] Some two weeks earlier, he had objected vehemently to the proposal that the forts in the Powder River Country be abandoned, because such action would leave "all the adventurous pioneers at the mercy of the redskin cut-throats."[106] The *Montana Post* agreed, labeling the members of the Peace Commission (except for General Sherman) as "corrupt or visionary ninnies."[107]

Public agitation for military action against the Indians of the northern plains is well represented by the following "Memorial and Joint Resolution of the Legislative Assembly of the Territory of Wyoming, Feb. 23, 1876," addressed to the Congress of the United States.

> While all the power of the Government has been threatened, and in a sense used, to prevent white men from trespassing on their lands, so uselessly held by them to the exclusion of those who would mine for precious metals (which it is well known exist there) these lawless pets have been allowed to leave their reservations (so called) whenever they would, to prey upon and devastate the property, lives, and peaceful occupations of these frontier settlers, with the property, lives and peaceful occupations of these frontier settlers, with the virtual consent of their guardians, the agents of the Government. While the blood-seeking brave (God save the word!) and his filthy squaw have fed at the public expense in those hatch-holes of fraud known as agencies, the widow and children of the white man slain by the treacherous Indian have been obliged to depend on their own energies or the bounty of neighbors for the necessaries of life. . . .
>
> In behalf of a long-suffering people . . . we would ask that the Indians shall be removed from us entirely, or else made amenable to the common law of the land. . . .
>
> We ask that our delegate . . . may be listened to and heeded with at least as much respect as some Indian-loving fanatic of the East. . . .[108]

Recommendations for resort to force also emanated from the Indian Service. In 1867, Indian Superintendent Hampton B. Denman suggested strongly to the Commissioner, "Either make a treaty, giving up to them the exclusive occupation of the country . . . or send troops enough . . . to scour the whole country, and either exterminate the greater part of the hostile Indians or drive them from it."[109] In 1872, Commissioner Francis J. Walker said it was federal policy that "the Indians should be made as comfortable on, and as uncomfortable off, their reservations as it was in the power of the government to make them; that such of them as went right should be protected and fed, and such as went wrong should be harassed and scourged without intermission."[110] Finally, according to the November 9, 1875, report of U.S. Indian Inspector E. C. Watkins, "The true policy . . . is to send troops against them [Sioux] in the winter — the sooner the better — and whip them into subjection."[111] As subsequent events demonstrated, this policy advice was, within the next few years, followed.

Senator Doolittle, in reporting on a visit to the site of Black Kettle's camp on Sand Creek, philosophized "that while it may be hard to make an Indian into a civilized white man, it is not so difficult a thing to make white men into Indian savages."[112] We approach more closely to the truth by eliminating racial identity from the Senator's statement. Developing and sustaining civilized behavior is more difficult than many assume, and more easily lost than some are willing to admit.

Retaining cultural curiosity, reducing confusion, moving away from contempt and conceit — all lower the likelihood of conflict and represent steps toward "civilized" behavior, properly defined. In the past, a number of peoples have approximated this type of behavior *within* their own groups; the record of "civilizing" intergroup relations is much more dismal. Within this context, perhaps Justice Holmes spoke wisely on another point. Programs, policies, legislation, and laws can only truly succeed to the extent that all of us become more "civilized."

Notes

1 Mark DeWolfe Howe, ed., *Holmes-Pollock Letters* (Cambridge: Harvard University Press, 1941), vol. 1, p. 122. Cited in Samuel J. Konefsky, *The Legacy of Holmes and Brandeis: A Study in the Influence of Ideas* (New York: Collier Books, 1956), p. 14.

2 "Diary of John Ball," copied from the *Oregon Historical Quarterly*, vol. 3, no. 1, by Devere Helfrich. Entry from July 9 (1832). Unless otherwise noted, this and other similarly designated diary citations refer to typed copies in the files of Mr. Paul Henderson, Bridgeport, Nebraska.

3 Albert J. Partoll, ed., "Anderson's Narrative of a Ride to the Rocky Mountains in 1834," *Frontier and Midland*, Autumn, 1938, p. 61. Hereafter referred to as "Anderson's Narrative."

4 Harry N. M. Winton, ed., "William Thompson Newby's Diary of the Emigration of 1843," copied from the *Oregon Historical Quarterly*, September, 1939, by Devere Helfrich. Entry for August 23. Hereafter referred to as "Newby's Diary."

5 Edwin Bryant, *What I Saw In California*, entry for July 14 (1846), p. 75.

6 Charles Kelly, ed., "The Journal of Robert Chalmers, April 17-September 1, 1850," The *Utah Historical Quarterly*, January, 1952. Entry for June 7, p. 40. Hereafter referred to as "The Journal of Robert Chalmers."

[7]"Diary of Mrs. E. A. Hadley, Across in 1852," Entry for Friday, May 30, p. 9. The original of this diary is in a private museum of pioneer relics in Lake View, Oregon.

[8]"Diary of Lorenzo Dow Young," *Utah Historical Quarterly*, January-October, 1946. Entry for Monday, 24 (May, 1847), p. 159.

[9]"Journal of Henry Allyn, 1853," as copied from the *Transactions of the Forty-ninth Annual Reunion of the Oregon Pioneers Association*, Portland, June 16, 1921. Entry for June 14.

[10]"Diary of Asahel Munger and Wife." Entry for Friday, 31 (May, 1839).

[11]Oswald F. Wagner, "Lutheran Zealots Among the Crows," *Montana, The Magazine of Western History*, April, 1972. Entry for August 2, 1858, pp. 8-9. (Diary of Johann Schmidt.) Hereafter referred to as the "Diary of Johann Schmidt."

[12]Edwin Bryant, *op. cit.*, entry for July 14 (1846), p. 75.

[13]*Ibid.*, entry for June 23 (1846), pp. 57-58.

[14]George Keller, *A Trip Across the Plains and Life in California.* (Massillon: White's Press, 1851), p. 12.

[15]David M. Kiefer, "Over Barren Plains and Rock-Bound Mountains: Being the journal of a tour by the Overland Route and South Pass of the Rocky Mountains, across the Great Basin and through California, with incidents and scenes of the homeward voyage, in the years 1850 and 1851, by Adam Mercer Brown of Pittsburgh." *Montana, The Magazine of Western History*, October, 1972. Entry for June 6th, 1850, p. 20. Hereafter referred to as "Diary of Adam Brown."

[16]"Journal of Pierson Barton Reading, In His Journey of One Hundred Twenty-Three Days Across The Rocky Mountains From Westport On the Missouri River, 450 Miles Above St. Louis, to Monterey, California, On the Pacific Ocean, In 1843." *Quarterly of the Society of California Pioneers*, September, 1930. Entry for Saturday, June 17th, pp. 157-158. Hereafter referred to as "Journal of Pierson Barton Reading."

[17]Chas. D. Ferguson, *Experiences of a Forty-niner* (Cleveland, 1888) (Newberry Microfilm 4-1), compiler M. J. Mattes, 1945; transcriber Louise Ridge, 1946, p. 2.

[18]George Keller, *op. cit.*, p. 11.

[19]Robert L. Munkres, "The Plains Indian Threat on the Oregon Trail Before 1860." *Annals of Wyoming*, October 1968, p. 218.

[20]John C. Paige, "Wichita Indian Agents, 1857-1869," *Journal of the West*, July 1973, p. 406.

[21]*Ibid.*, p. 407.

[22]"Thomas Twiss to Col. Cumming, Supt. Indian Affairs," dated

Indian Agency, Fort Laramie, Dec. 25th, 1855. *Records of the Bureau of Indian Affairs, Selected Documents Concerning the Administration of Indian Affairs at the Upper Platte Indian Agency,* Record Group 75. Hereafter referred to as Record Group 75. It might be noted that Twiss also said that frontier Whites were not "the true and real white man," nor were they "the best specimens."

23T. A. Larson, ed., "Across the Plains in 1864 With George Forman: A Traveler's Account," *Annals of Wyoming,* April 1968. Entry for June 16th, pp. 10-11. Hereafter referred to as "Account of George Forman."

24Chas. D. Ferguson, *op. cit.,* p. 4.

25*Ibid.*

26"Henry E. Maynadier, Col 5th US Vols, Com'd'g, to Hon. D. N. Cooley, Commissioner of Indian Affairs, Washington, D.C." Dated Head Quarters West Sub District of Nebraska, Fort Laramie, D.T., March 9th 1866. Record Group 75.

27"Anderson's Narrative," *op. cit.,* p. 63.

28William Chandless, *Visit to Salt Lake.* London, 1857. (Newberry Microfilm 2-17), compiler M. J. Mattes, 1945; transcriber Louise Ridge, 1945, p. 10.

29Chas. D. Ferguson, *op. cit.,* p. 4.

30John T. Kearns, "Journal of Crossing the Plains to Oregon in 1852," as copied from the *Transactions of the Forty-Second Annual Reunion of the Oregon Pioneers Association,* Portland, Oregon, June 25, 1914. Entry for Sunday, July 4.

31"Diary of Adam Brown," *op cit.,* for April 26, 1850, p. 18. Whites were, apparently, particularly upset by the sight of Indian women "picking the vermin off another's head, and eating them with evident gusto."

32"Diary of Mrs. E. A. Hadley", entry for Monday, May 5th (1851).

33*Ibid.,* entry for Wednesday, May 7th (1851).

34"Diary of Dr. Benjamin Cory, Crossing the Plains." Entry for May 5 (1847).

35"Journal of Pierson Barton Reading," entry for Sunday 28th (May 1843), p. 150.

36"Diary of James Frear," entry for Wednesday, 12 May (1852).

37"Journal of Peter Skene Ogden: Snake Expedition, 1826-27," copied from the *Oregon Historical Quarterly,* vol. 2, no. 2 by Devere Helfrich. Entry for Monday 13 (February 1827).

38"Thomas Fitzpatrick to Thomas H. Harvey, Supert Indian Affairs," dated Bents Fort, Arkansas River, Oct. 19th, 1847. Record Group 75.

³⁹ "Thomas Fitzpatrick, Ind. Ag. Upper Platte to Lt. Col. Wm Gilpin, Comd Batt Plains, Missouri Vol." Dated Bents Fort, Arkansas River, Feb. 10, 1848. Record Group 75. During this era, some advanced the theory of separate creation as the explanation of presumed Indian inferiority. *Types of Mankind* by J. C. Nott and George R. Gliddon, for example, contained the following statement: "To one who has lived among American Indians, it is in vain to talk of civilizing them. . . . You might as well attempt to change the nature of the buffalo." Cited in Brian W. Dippie, "This Bold But Wasting Race: Stereotypes and American Indian Policy," *Montana, The Magazine of Western History,* Janaury 1973, p. 8.

⁴⁰ Milton E. Holtz, "Old Fort Kearney — 1846-1848: Symbol of a Changing Frontier," *Montana, The Magazine of Western History,* October 1972, p. 48. Other tribes were, of course, mentioned specifically. For instance, Snakes "are the most thieving Indians on the road" ("Diary of E. W. Conyers, A Pioneer of 1852," as copied from the *Transactions of the Thirty-Third Annual Reunion of the Oregon Pioneer Association,* June 15, 1905, Entry for July 9, Friday). "northern Cheyennes' from the Powder River Country . . . are the most horrid looking creatures of all the Indians that I have seen . . . looking in all respects like fiends" (Donald K. Adams, ed., "The Journal of Ada A. Vogdes, 1868-71," *Montana, The Magazine of Western History,* July 1963. Entry for 2 April 1870, p. 10); and "Digger Indians . . . [ære] the most miserable specimens of the red race our eyes ever rested upon" ("Diary of Adam Brown," entry for July 23rd (1850), p. 24).

⁴¹ "Diary of E. W. Conyers," entry for May 24, Monday (1852).

⁴² "Diary of John Ball," entry for September 17 (1832).

⁴³ E. S. McComas, *A Journal of Travel* (Portland, Ore.: Champoeg Press, 1954). Entry for 4th (July 1862).

⁴⁴ "Diary of Jason Lee," copied from the *Oregon Historical Quarterly* for 1916, vol. 17, by Devere Helfrich. Entry for Mon. 19 (May, 1834).

⁴⁵ Edwin Bryant, *op. cit.,* entry for June 1, (1846).

⁴⁶ J. Quinn Thornton, *Oregon and California in 1848* (New York: Harper & Brothers, 1864), entry for June 7th (1848) Sabbath, p. 24.

⁴⁷ Wm. G. Johnston, *Experiences of a Forty-Niner* (Pittsburgh, 1892), microfilmed 7-17-42 by the Library of Congress Photoduplication Service). Entry for Tuesday, May 15 (1849), pp. 90-91. Among others, Asa Brown (1850), Henry Allyn (1853), and Richard Thomas Ackley (1858) all used such terms as hostile, treacherous, cunning, and thievish to describe Pawnees.

⁴⁸ Mrs. Velina A. Williams, "Diary of a Trip Across the Plains in 1853," as copied from the *Transactions of the Forty-Seventh Annual Reunion of the Oregon Pioneers Association,* Portland, June 19,

1919. Entry for May 24 (1853).

49 *Ibid.*

50 C. W. Smith, *Journal of a Trip to California: Across the Continent From Weston, Mo., to Weber Creek, Cal., In the Summer of 1850.* Edited and with an Introduction and Notes by R.W.G. Vail (New York: Theicadmus Book Shop; Manchester, N.H.: Press Standard Book Company), entry for May 22 (1850).

51 "D. D. Mitchell, Supt. Ind Affs' to Hon L. Lea Com. Ind. Affairs," dated Office Supt. Indian Affairs, St. Louis, November 11th 1851. Record Group 75.

52 "Thomas Twiss to Commissioner of Indian Affairs," dated Camp of the Indian Agency at Raw Hide Creek, Nov. 13th, 1856. Record Group 75.

53 "Henry Heth, Lieut 6th Infantry, Comdg Post to Capt. J. McDowell, Assist. Adjt. General. 6 Mily Dept. Jefferson Barracks, Missouri," dated Head Quarters Fort Atkinson, Santa Fe Route, April 14, 1853. Record Group 75.

54 "J. A. Cody, United States Indian Agent, Upper Platte to Hon. Wm. P. Dole, Commissioner of Indian Affairs," dated United States Indian Agency, Upper Platte Near Fort Laramie, Nebraska Territory December 18, 1861. Record Group 75.

55 J. Quinn Thornton, *op. cit.*, entry for June 7th (1846), p. 25.

56 Theodore Talbot, *Journals* (Newberry Microfilm: 2-11), compiler M. J. Mattes, 1945; transcriber Louise Ridge, 1945. Entry for Wednesday, 2d (August 1843).

57 "Thomas Fitzpatrick to Thomas H. Harvey, Supert. Indian Affairs," dated Bents Fort, Arkansas River, Oct. 19th, 1847. Record Group 75.

58 *Ibid.*

59 "Thomas Fitzpatrick, Ind. Ag. to Hon. W. Medill, Commd. Ind. Affrs.," dated Washington City, August 11th, 1848.

60 *Ibid.*

61 Gary L. Roberts, "Condition of the Tribes — 1865, The McCook Report: A Military View," *Montana, The Magazine of Western History,* January 1974, p. 22. Hereafter referred to as "The McCook Report." To the statement reproduced above, General McCook added "and the want of discipline in the volunteer forces serving on the Plains," one evidence of which was the failure of officers to punish men who "commit personal outrages on Indians. . . ." (p. 23). The other major cause cited by the general was "the almost universal bad faith of Indian Agents toward Indians in defrauding them out of the annuities and presents granted them by law."

62 Tony McGinnis, "Economic Warfare on the Northern Plains, 1804-1877," *Annals of Wyoming* Spring, 1972, pp. 57-58.

[63] With admirably consistent short-sightedness, some Whites solicited Indian military assistance against traditional tribal enemies. After the purposes of government policy had been served, however, the same individuals frequently became upset because the Indians would not willingly stop the war!

[64] It can be noted that Thomas Hobbes, one of the creators of the modern doctrine of sovereignty did not assume that subjects would do much "negotiating" with their sovereign in Leviathan! Perhaps Indians interpreted the fictional filial relationship embodied in much treaty terminology more on the basis of the roles of fathers, i.e., elders, within the context of Indian society. If they did so, then confusion was simply compounded.

[65] In December of 1855, the President, through Secretary of War Jefferson Davis, authorized General Harney "to make a convention or treaty for the restoration of friendly relations with such of the chiefs and head men of the respective tribes of the Sioux *as may be duly empowered to act with you*" (italics added). It is at least questionable to assume that any Indian leader was "duly empowered to act" in the legal sense in which the phrase was apparently being used. (Jeff Davis, Secretary of War to Brevet Brig General W. S. Harney, U.S. Army, Comdg Sioux Expedition, Fort Pierre, *via* Council Bluffs, Iowa," dated War Department, Washington Dec. 26, 1855. Record Group 75.

[66] It is interesting to note that Indian culture came reasonably close to the concept of property ownership described by John Locke as existing in a "State of Nature," i.e., ownership results from the mixture of an individual's labor with the resources of nature which are held in common.

[67] "Thomas Fitzpatrick, Ind Agt, Upper Platte & Arkansas to A Cummings Esqr Sup Ind Affairs at St Louis," dated Saint Louis, Missouri, Nov. 19th, 1853. Record Group 75.

[68] "Ashton S. H. White to Hon. O. H. Browning, Secretary of the Interior, Washington, D.C.," dated Fort Laramie, D.T., April 14th 1868. Record Group 75.

[69] "Thomas Fitzpatrick to Thomas H. Harvey, Supert Indian Affairs," dated Bents Fort, Arkansas River, Oct. 19th, 1847. Record Group 75.

[70] "Ed Johnson, Pvt. Maj. & Capt. 6th Infy., Comg to Capt. T. N. Page, Asst. Adjt. Genl, 6th Mil. Dept., Jefferson Barracks, Mo.," dated Head Quarters, Fort Atkinson, Santa Fe Route Sept 10th 1853. Record Group 75.

[71] "Felix R. Brunot, Chm Board of Indian Commissioners and Robt. Campbell to Hon J D Cox, Secretary of the Interior, Washington, D.C.," dated Department of the Interior, Board of Indian Commissioners, Pittsburgh, Oct. 19th, 1870. Record Group 75.

[72] "E.B. Taylor, Supt Ind Affairs to Hon D.N. Cooley, Commissioner

Indian Affairs," dated Washington, August 23, 1866. Record Group 75. Later in the same letter, Mr. Taylor referred to news coming out of Leavenworth as deriving from "the fertile imagination of some enterprising gentleman who cares more for army contracts than the public peace."

73 "The McCook Report," p. 18.

74 "The Journal of Robert Chalmers," entry for May 11 (1850), p. 36.

75 "Journal of Henry Allyn, 1853," entry for May 19-Thursday.

76 "Minutes and report of a sub-commission of the Board of Indian Commissioners composed of Felix R. Brunot, Chairman of the board and Robert Campbell. Conference with the Utes," dated Sept. 5, 1870. Record Group 75.

77 "Jeffn. Davis, Secretary of War to the President.," dated War Department, Washington, May 31, 1856. Record Group 75.

78 "Alf Sully, Bvt. Brig. Genl. Presdt of Commission to Hon N.G. Taylor, Commissioner Indian Affairs," dated Fort Berthold D.T., June 22d, 1867. Record Group 75.

79 "Vital Jarrot, U.S. Ind. Agent to Hon D.N. Cooley," dated Omaha, Nebraska, Oct 5th, 1865. Record Group 75.

80 "Thomas Fitzpatrick, Ind. Ag. Upper Platte to Lt. Col. Wm Gilpin, Comd Batt Plains, Missouri Vol," dated Bents Fort, Arkansas River, Feb. 10, 1848. Record Group 75. Mitchell thought that "fifty years . . . would be time sufficient to give the experiment a fair trial" to see if a treaty system could be made to work. ("D.D. Mitchell, Supt. Ind Affs' to Hon L. Lea Com. Ind. Affairs," dated Office Supt. Indian Affairs., St. Louis, November 11th 1851. Record Group 75.

81 Brigadier General James H. Carleton. Cited in Richard C. Hopkins, "Kit Carson and the Navajo Expedition," *Montana, The Magazine of Western History* April 1968, p. 55.

82 "The McCook Report," p.23.

83 *Congressional Record, 43rd Congress, 2nd Session,* vol. 3, Part 1, Dec. 7, 1874-Jan. 28, 1875 (Washington, D.C.: Government Printing Office), p. 461.

84 D. S. Otis, *The Dawes Act and the Allotment of Indian Lands.* Edited with an Introduction by Francis Paul Prucha (Norman, Okla.: University of Oklahoma Press, 1973), p. 10.

85 *Ibid.,* p. 11.

86 "Thomas Fitzpatrick to Thomas H. Harvey, Supert Indian Affairs," dated Bents Fort, Arkansas River, Oct. 19th, 1847. Record Group 75. He was also very dubious about the proposition that only "the introduction of Christianity was wanting to make them [Indians] happy and prosperous.

[87]Gene M. Gressley, ed., "A Cattleman Views Indian Policy — 1875," *Montana, The Magazine of Western History* January 1967, p. 11.

[88]Donald N. Wells, "Farmers Forgotten: Nez Perce Suppliers of the North Idaho Gold Rush Days," *Journal of the West* July 1972, p. 492.

[89]"N. S. Clarke, Col 6 Infy, Brv't. Brig General, Commanding to Colonel L. Thomas, Assistant Adjutant General, Head Quarters of the Army, New York," dated Head Quarters, Department of the West, Jefferson Barracks, October 5, 1854. Record Group 75.

[90]A man named Foote killed an Indian. The agent suggested "that they [the Indians] be rewarded with a suitable present and that Foote and Hunter be ordered out of the Indian Country. . . . Should you think of any other plan which would give satisfaction to the Indians please do so." ("John Loree, Ind Agent to W.O. Collins, Lt Col Comdg, Ft. Laramie," dated Upper Platte Agency, July 18th 1864. Record Group 75.

[91]"Journal of Peter Skene Ogden: Snake Expedition, 1826-27," entry for Friday, 10th Feb. (1827).

[92]"Thomas Fitzpatrick, Ind. Ag. to Hon. W. Medill, Commd. Ind. Affrs.," dated Washington City, August 11th 1848. Record Group 75.

[93]". W. Thissel, *Crossing the Plains in '49*. Oakland, 1903. (Newberry Microfilm 3-8) Compiler M. J. Mattes, 1945. Transcriber Louise Ridge, 1946. Entry for May 21, 1950.

[94]"Overland Journal of John McGlashen — 1850," entry for May 5th. Two points must be noted in conjunction with Indian hostility toward wagon trains. One, a majority of emigrants never experienced an open attack by Indians. Two, while most emigrants were armed, a great many of them were hardly expert in the use of their weapons. As a result of the latter, firearms accidents were not unusual and, among other things, blankets, mules, rocks, and other emigrants were mistaken for Indians and fired upon.

[95]Paul Bonnifield, "The Choctaw Nation on the Eve of the Civil War," *Journal of the West* July 1973, p. 391.

[96]Watson Parker, "The Majors and the Miners: The Role of the U.S. Army in the Black Hills Gold Rush," *Journal of the West* January 1972, p. 99. Some Indian leaders subsequently became aware of the impact of white population increases. In 1870, Red Cloud stated the Indians' dilemma with elegant simplicity: "The whites' children have surrounded me & have left me nothing but an island. When we first had this land we were strong. Now we are melting like snow on the hill side while you are growing like spring grass." ("Interview with Red Cloud: United States Special Commission. June 7th 1870." Record Group 75.)

[97]"The McCook Report," p. 23. The General also urged "that the Indian Bureau cease to exist, and that all matters pertaining to

Indian affairs be transferred to the War Dept., where they were originally and where they now belong." *Ibid.*, p. 24.

98 *Ibid.*, p. 24.

99"W.T. Sherman, General to General C.C. Augur, Omaha, Nebraska (Telegram)," dated Headquarters of the Army, Washington, May 12, 1870. Record Group 75.

100"W.T. Sherman, General to Lieutenant General P.H. Sheridan, Helena, Montana (Telegram)," dated Headquarters Army of the United States, Washington, D.C., May 18, 1870. Record Group 75.

101 *Ibid.*

102 *Ibid.*

103Eugene V. McAndrews, "An Army Engineer's Journal of Custer's Black Hills Expedition, July 2, 1874-August 23, 1874," *Journal of the West* January 1974, p. 84.

104 *Ibid.*, pp. 84-85. It should not be assumed from the foregoing tha the frontier army particularly desired military confrontation with Indians. After the Sioux War of 1876, General Crook spoke to his troops in the following manner: "Indian warfare is, of all warfare, the most trying and the most thankless. . . . It possesses for you all the disadvantages of civilized warfare, with all the horrible accompaniment that barbarism can invent and savages execute. In it you are required to serve without the incentive of promotion or recognition, in truth, without favor or hope of reward. . . ." (Watson Parker, *op. cit.*, p. 113.)

105James C. Murphy, "The Place of the Northern Arapahoes in the Relations Between the United States and the Indians of the Plains, 1851-1879," *Annals of Wyoming* April 1969, p. 42.

106Gene Gressley, *op. cit.*, p. 4.

107A. Glen Humpherys, "The Crow Indian Treaties of 1868: An Example of Power Struggle and Confusion in United States Indian Policy," *Annals of Wyoming* Spring 1971, p. 85.

108James C. Murphy, *op. cit.*, p. 43.

109Jerome A. Green, "The Hayfield Fight: A Reappraisal of a Neglected Action," *Montana, The Magazine of Western History* October 1972, p. 42.

110Lois L. Nelsen Schmidlin, "The Role of the Horse in the Life of the Comanche," *Journal of the West* January 1974, p. 62.

111William A. Dobak, "Yellow-Leg Journalists: Enlisted Men as Newspaper Reporters in the Sioux Campaign, 1876," *Journal of the West* January 1974, p. 89.

112"The McCook Report," *op. cit.*, p. 20.

The Reservation Indian Meets The White Man (1860-1914)

Joseph H. Cash, University of South Dakota

It should be recognized from the outset that any attempt to discuss the "reservation Indian" in his meetings with the "white man" during a time frame that runs from the pre-reservation period on the northern plains to World War I is open to the most blatant of generalizations, and the unwary historian is certain to be picked apart in detail. This unwary historian fully understands that the meeting of two dynamic cultures depends upon more variables than can be properly investigated here. Put in its simplest form, everything depends upon which Indian met which white man at what time and under what particular set of circumstances. If this somewhat amorphous state can be accepted, certain patterns can be discerned and perhaps a basis of interpretation begun.

The most spectacular arena where the Indians met the white men from 1860 to 1890 was on the field of battle. The white man, and particularly the United States Army, was sporadically a major adversary of the Plains Indians during all this period. The record of the clashes is all too familiar. The great Sioux Wars of Minnesota in 1862 and the Sand Creek Massacre in Colorado in 1864 are illustrative of battles that broke out as a result of the confusion of the Civil War period and the resulting use of amateurs by the United States Army. It is astounding that the Plains Indians understood as well as they did the breakdown of the American military, as well as the breakdown of the administration of Indian affairs during the Civil War. Yet, seen another way, it is less surprising. The Indian, a notable warrior himself, had a feel and a touch for the capacity, courage, and honor of his adversary.

When the disorganization of the Civil War ended and the Plains became an area penetrated, instead of merely crossed, trouble increased and culminated in the Custer fight on the Little Big Horn in 1876. This time, combined tribes fought the regular United States Army instead of rag-tag units put together out of local volunteers and commanded by men who sometimes, as in the case of the Methodist preacher, Chivington, exhibited almost pathological tendencies toward slaughter. It became a situation of pro versus pro, and respect was frequently exhibited between the two.

Thus it was that the Plains Indians tended to respect the American soldier, the white man in uniform, as he deserved respect. Chivington of Colorado was despised, yet feared. Custer, who won his first reputation as an Indian fighter by his sneak attack on the Cheyennes at the Washita, was referred to as "the skulking coyote." He was a man who would not fight with honor, but chose to attack at daybreak during a tough winter and indiscriminately kill women and children. This latter tendency was always a sore spot with the Indians and a source of their weakness. Possessing no professional army, they usually had to react to the advances of American forces against them under situations where wives and children were very close at hand. They did not consider their women and children to be logical targets of war, and they despised the United States soldiers who did. In their own intertribal wars, of course, women and children were killed, but never deliberately. Capture was more frequent; the women became wives or slaves and the children were reared as tribal members in the victor's camp. A deliberate policy of wiping out innocents did not appeal to them. Sheridan's famous comment that "nits make lice," which some took as a license for killing children, was foreign to the Indians; they despised the white man who did it. In truth, most white men did not do it. There are many touching instances of the charitable and honorable behavior of white soldiers to the wives and children of the fallen enemies.

The later Indian wars that resulted in the rounding up of the Sioux and other so-called hostile people required better soldiers to command the striking forces. Generals like Nelson Miles and George Crook were men of honor, and they treated their opponents accordingly. The Indians respected them; indeed, many of the Indian names that have the term "Star" in them were given in honor of white soldiers. The Three Stars family is descended from a child named after George Crook. There are other instances which show the respect of the Indian for an honorable opponent. For example, Spotted Tail's daughter dreamed of marrying an army officer. When she died, he took her to Fort Laramie where the Army buried her with high military honors. The sorrowing father appreciated this and viewed soldiers with respect and gratitude. Even on the tragic battlefield of Wounded Knee, there is evidence that some of the surviving Indians blamed their Medicine Man, Yellow Bird, more than they did the Army. There are instances of white soldiers rearing Indian children orphaned by that tragic affair. Even Kit Carson, who badly defeated the Navajo and relocated them, was not accorded hatred or dishonor by the people he had beaten. They knew him. They knew what kind of a man he was. They could understand his doing his duty as he saw it. Indeed, one may say that the fraternity of the fighting man frequently overcame the hostility of two cultures meeting in violent embrace.

It is usually overlooked that while many Indians fought the white man on and off from 1860 until 1880, other Indian tribes allied with the Whites and became important adjuncts to the United States of America. The participation of Crow and Arikara scouts with Custer's command on June 26, 1876, is well known. Less known is the alliance of the remnants of the Mandan, Arikara, and Hidatsa with the United States during this entire period, or of the close ties between the Pawnee and the United States at the same time. One may wonder why the American Indians would ally with the people who were taking over their territory. The answer is simple: they chose the lesser of two evils. They sought an ally in the face of almost certain destruction emanating from neighboring Indian tribes. The outlines of the situation of each of these tribes is instructive.

The Crow had been subject to intense military pressure for most of the 19th century. Driven out of western South Dakota, they established a homeland that was centered near the headwaters of the Yellowstone upward toward the Missouri in what is now the state of Montana. They had bitter and determined enemies on nearly all sides. To the northwest were the Blackfeet, who raided them and who were in turn raided on a continuing basis. To the south lived the Utes and Northern Cheyenne — always enemies. Due north were the Assiniboines, also enemies; to the southeast, the Sioux, who were called by the Crow, "They who cut off our heads." To the west were Shoshone and Nez Perce, with whom they fought and traded sporadically. Their only Indian allies were their former tribesmen, the Hidatsa, and the Mandan and Arikara. These three, heavily decimated by smallpox and themselves under severe attack by the Sioux, were in litttle position to help. The Crow were surrounded and isolated by a number of tribes that would have delighted in wiping them out. At stake was perhaps the best Indian country in North America. Absaroke, the land of the Crow, possessed good grass, plenty of water, and the last hard-core areas of the northern buffalo. The Crow turned to the white man to help because there was no alternative. It was not a case of affection, but of necessity. Churchill, when allying with the Russians in World War II, made a remark to the effect that he would ally with Satan if it would help beat Hitler. The Crow would ally with anybody who could offer them protection. They did not regard the white men as being blood brothers, and they may have actually disliked them more than did the Sioux. There were constant complaints from the Crow that they got less for good behavior than the Sioux got for outright hostility. The same complaint came from every other tribe that allied with the United States government against other Indians. Apparently the rule of the squeaking wheel getting the grease had some truth in this situation. More rations, better land deals, and finer presents went to Indians who were hostile. The ones that were friendly got what was left — and they didn't like it. Yet, there were many white men whom they did admire — some traders, some army officers, and some missionaries. Above all, they were trapped in their situation and, as the weaker member of a partnership, learned to expect less than they deserved and get less than they earned. On the other hand, all evidence points to the fact that they knew that survival depended on the alliance with the Whites and that loving an ally was not necessary. They sought survival and achieved it through their alliances.

The Pawnee had the same situation. Driven far south by the Brulé Sioux, they were subject to periodic and decimating attacks. Sioux warriors rode through Pawnee earth-lodge villages time after time. As late as 1873, a number of Pawnee on a hunt were ambushed by Spotted Tail and his Brulés. They were forced to an uneasy alliance with the United States, and blue-coated soldiers saved the remnants of that unhappy tribe.

Above all, the Three Affiliated Tribes, the Mandan, Hidatsa, and Arikara, felt the pressure of the Sioux. Huddled around Fort Berthold, they came under constant attack. In the 1870s, the question was never whether the Sioux would attack, but when. The Yanktonai, Hunkpapa, and most of the northern divisions of the Tetons came at them hard and often, putting them in a position of near beggarhood. The pressure was so intense that they could no longer feed themselves and were totally dependent on the United States. There was less respect for the Americans than for the fighting tribes opposing them. They were so totally dependent, so far up the Missouri, so lacking in resources, that they took what they could get, and it usually wasn't much. They were in a desparate situation and would undoubtedly have been totally wiped out if it hadn't been for the United States Government. They appreciated any help and fought beside the Army. Bloody Knife, of the Arikara, was Custer's favorite scout. These people constantly complained, however, because the sight of their sworn enemies receiving more for behaving badly disturbed them immensely.

Throughout this period, there seemed to have been very little to be gained by allying with the United States. Their rations were no better. When the time came, the rations were allotted, the reservations were reduced, and key areas were penetrated by the white man to about the same degree as for those who had chosen to fight. Yet, the policy of alliance with the white man was necessary. Survival is always the first priority of any people, but it does not necessarily insure a glorious future and the gratitude of those you have helped.

The Indian met the white man on a fairly regular basis at the negotiating table. It might be on matters of state wherein special commissions sent out from Washington would attempt to get a favorable treaty or a land cession from the Indian. It might be a local affair where a sub-chief would meet with the agency superintendent, or it might be the ordinary Indian meeting with the ordinary bureaucrat over a matter of private interest. Regardless of the level of negotiation, meet they did; in these meetings, which went on from 1860 to 1914, the Indians had a good chance to judge the Wasicu.

On the most elemental level, that of the individual Indian vis-à-vis the minor bureaucrat, both were subject to extreme frustration. The bureaucrat was hemmed in by rules, regulations, and instructions over which he had no control. The

Indians, on the other hand, were concerned with their property rights, and they desired an ideal form of justice. Ideal justice seldom comes from lower level bureaucrats, and the complaints of the Indians through the years were long and onstant. From the reports of Indian commissioners and agency superintendents down to contemporary interviews, the theme runs true and constant — frustration. The Indians respected strength, honor, integrity, and immediateness of response. They could even respect this when it worked against them. They despised the men who retreated to the book of regulations that they could not read, could not understand, and were indisposed to learn. There were times, particularly prior to the twentieth century, when their frustration led to contempt, which in turn could lead to minor acts of violence. In the twentieth century, it more often led to the sneer and the impassive turning of the back as the proud Indian male stalked from the door preferring to forego his case rather than continue an exercise in trivia. The result was the loss of many rights and much property as the tribesman failed to defend his own by the white man's rules. The same held true in legal cases, particularly those dealing with the criminal courts. Following the passing of the Major Crime Act in 1882, many convictions of Indians came from either guilty pleas or a failure to defend with the vigor that the ordinary white man would have exhibited. Again, lack of understanding and contempt for legalistic formality, as well as natural reserve, led to many unwarranted and undeserved sentences. It is difficult to blame the bureaucrats or the judges. They, too, were tied into a system that they did not originate, but that they were sworn to uphold. Such men could not be expected to catch every nuance of a difficult acculturation during its most controversial phases.

On the level of the chief and the agent, it depended on who the chief was and who the agent was. A man like Red Cloud on Pine Ridge was strong enough to have had a war named after him, and continually made life hell for his agents. He was discriminating — the stronger the agent, the harder Red Cloud went after him. When Dr. Valentine McGillicudy was on Pine Ridge, the battle achieved epic proportions. McGillicudy, as strong in character as Red Cloud himself and a man who had once faced the famed chief down, took on Red Cloud head to head. There was threat and counterthreat, bluff and counterbluff, move and countermove, sometimes emanating from one, sometimes from the other. McGillicudy used his Indian police, threatened to use the army, and manipulated rations. Red Cloud faked warriors' attacks on the agency. When he went east on his frequent trips to visit the Great White Father, he complained bitterly of the man in charge of the agency. He was never able to get rid of McGillicudy — patronage during a political change eventually did that — but he was able to get him investigated and keep him worried. While on the surface there was sheer hatred, one suspects that beneath it all there was a grudging respect on the part of both men.

There were easier agents. The man in charge of Pine Ridge in 1890 was so weak that the Oglalas referred to him as "the agent who is afraid of us." Such men aroused contempt. Again, the Indian ideal of strength in a leader was shown. On Standing rock, James McLaughlin had weaknesses, but cowardice was not among them. He, in turn, fought with a noted Indian — in this case, Sitting Bull. As an unintended result of his orders, a situation arose wherein the famed medicine man was killed. Yet, McLaughlin went onward and upward in the Indian Service and would later write a book entitled, *My Friend, the Indian* . Alas, Sitting Bull was not alive to review it.

On the Rosebud Reservation, Spotted Tail never had an agent he could not get along with — one way or another. This was due more to the diplomatic skills of the chief than it was to the quality of the agents. Spotted Tail took men as he found them and manipulated them to his own purposes. He was exceptional at it. The Henry Kissinger of the Red Man, Spotted Tail used threats, cajolery, diplomatic dissembling, and an exceptional mind to get what he desired. He did not always win, but he seldom came out with less than a draw.

When the age of the great chiefs ended in the '90's, life was easier for the government negotiators. There was no one with the stature, ability, and experience of a Red Cloud, a Spotted Tail, a Sitting Bull, a Gall. Death, old age, and government policy had weakened the institution of the chieftainship. With the buffalo gone and the Indian military power broken, the agency people had the Indians on the defensive and were quite ready to exploit this advantage as the situation — and the laws emanating from Washington — indicated.

The highest-level negotiations took place when treaties, agreements, and land cessions were on the line. The high stakes separated true leadership from mere forensics and required skill of the highest order. The chiefs who conducted the negotiations usually ended up losing something. Later generations have sometimes regarded them as being weak or as selling out. Nothing could be further from the truth. These leaders fought dogged battles against a superior foe across the negotiating table. They respected some of their white counterparts highly — more, they despised. A man like Newton D. Edmunds, sometime Governor of Dakota Territory, was noted as a negotiator of Indian treaties and agreements. He loved nothing better than to sally forth alone or with a commission to negotiate from his exalted position as ex-officio superintendent of Indian affairs for Dakota Territory. Agreements he got — some of them smelled so highly that the United States Senate, not a notably fastidious body in the 1800s, refused to ratify them. He was unloved by his Indian charges, who believed that he took unfair advantage in negotiations, and worst of all, that his agreement, once made, would not be fulfilled. In other words, Edmunds was regarded as a colossal liar. On the other hand, a man like General Crook (Three Stars, as the Indians knew him) was highly respected. Brave in battle, he was honorable in negotiations. He had endless patience in listening to the interminable Indian oratory. He laid out his position clearly and concisely and made it quite clear to the Indians that if they would not deal, they could fight. This sort of a man was respected and understood. The practice of saddling Crook with a commission made up of ex-Governors, second-rate Senators, and the like in 1889 points out the stature of the man. He still achieved the agreement of 1889, which superceded the Laramie Treaty of 1868. He later resigned his commission in the United States Army because he felt that the government had not lived up to the promises that he had made. He was a man of honor whom the Indians could and did respect.

By the time it came to allotting the northern plains reservations, usually the first decade of the twentieth century, the stature of negotiators on the white man's side meant little. The Indians by then had played their final card. They no longer had any real hope of holding onto their entire reservations. Rather, they concentrated on getting as good a price as possible. During the negotiations, there was an arrogance on the part of their white opponents that was unthinkable in the period of Indian power. It was not that evil men negotiated the agreements, and the Indians did not consider them such. There was, however, no

one of the stature of George Crook. There was a note of constantly rising impatience on the part of the white man that must
have bothered the Indians with their strong sense of the
proprieties of formal negotiation. The white man wanted a business deal, and the Indians wanted a diplomatic relationship —
both were disappointed. The reservations' land total was whit-
tled down, always with the best of motives and with the best interests of the red man at heart. By this time, however, there
was a contempt on the part of the white man and a resignation
on the part of the Indians that had been absent in earlier and
more glorious days. The record was sordid.

The ability of the Indians to know and respect their opponents depended on the character and strength of those opponents and on the strength of the Indians. As the basic power
balance altered, the need for serious and outstanding men like
Crook or Spotted Tail lessened. Mutual respect counted for less.
Strong men meant less. A people changing from proud armed
warriors to wards of the government were not likely to be happy. They blamed the only people they could blame — those that
they met — the agents and the negotiators. They should have
blamed the Congress and the people of the United States who
created their unhappy situation.

Throughout the entire period that the Indians were on
their reservations, and sometimes when they weren't, they
were subject to the administration of the United States Government operating through its chosen instrument, the Bureau of
Indian Affairs. Founded in 1834 as part of the War Department
and actually possessing a history going back to the beginnings
of the Republic, this Bureau was tied up in endless regulations,
forced to conduct policies that it did not make, and open to a dis-
like on the part of the American Indian that still exists. One
might pity its employees if it were possible to pity bureaucrats.
Certainly there were good and capable men among them, but
just as certainly the scent of corruption and assorted skulldug-
gery trailed the record of the Bureau down through the decades.
Even when innocent, people believed them guilty. Most important, the Indians believed it, and it is excessively difficult to
properly administer dubious programs in complex situations re-
quiring the cooperation of people who think you are a crook. As
anyone conversant with the news today can tell you, such situations are not confined to the Bureau of Indian Affairs or to
the nineteenth century. Yet, the BIA seems cursed with a

reputation for villainy that is unmatched. It mattered little whether the agent was a Quaker chosen by a church board, an Army officer with vast administrative skills, or a politician forced to the frontiers to recoup his fortunes. In most cases, the aroma penetrated the Bureau in such a permanent way that few of its members have been able to escape it. Even a man such as McGillicudy at Pine Ridge was subject to investigation, and numbers of people will still swear that he stole more than a quarter of a million dollars. It was never proved. Indeed, every investigation exonerated him completely. Yet, his name is sullied. McLaughlin of Standing Rock was seldom accused of being a crook. Better things were in store for him. He is frequently described as the murderer of Sitting Bull, although he was nowhere near the spot where Sitting Bull died, and those who were probably did not commit anything approaching murder. While McLaughlin was not exactly in tears over Sitting Bull's untimely demise, he certainly had not anticipated it. Yet, because he is tainted by his membership in the BIA, a great many people are still willing to believe the worst of him.

There were agents who did manage to lift things. Everyone's favorite was Walter Burleigh, an agent to the Yankton Sioux. His tenure in office barely took him into our period of interest, but he was such a total crook that he was engaging and lovable. The story is told that Burleigh, a native of Pennsylvania, had helped carry that state for Abraham Lincoln in 1860 and wanted the ambassadorship to the Court of St. James as his reward. Lincoln allowed as how that particular job was filled and how would Dr. Burleigh like to be agent to the Yankton Sioux? Burleigh, somewhat taken aback but always a man open to opportunity, inquired as to the salary. Lincoln replied, "$1,500 a year." Walter Burleigh explained, "Mr. Lincoln, at that salary, in that area, and with my family, I'll either have to starve or steal." To which Lincoln replied, "Dr. Burleigh, if I am any judge of character, you won't starve." And indeed he did not. He kept a long way from starvation, and in the words of George Washington Plunckett, "he seen his opportunities and he took 'em." He went on to become somewhat of a power in Dakota politics with strong railroad interests, and while the Yankton Sioux suffered, they too were rather astonished by this remarkable man and his legendary feats of skullduggery. Modern informants indicate that Burleigh was one of the best liked of the superintendents. Perhaps he appealed to the Indians' sense of humor. He certainly could not have appealed to any sense of respect that they possessed for the white man.

For all the gaudy examples, and there are many, that came from the administrative branch of the Bureau of Indian Affairs, the trend in the twentieth century was toward the faceless, formless bureaucrat — the gray little men who manned the pencils, the typewriters, and by our time, the computers. The major complaints changed from screams of anguish about being cheated to groans of pure boredom. The most familiar sight in any Bureau building was that of great numbers of people sitting and waiting. The line had replaced individual rage. Whether it was in the Land Office, the Loan Office, or in an Indian Service hospital, the impression was always of people waiting. The same faces were there day after day, week after week, trying to get someone to listen, trying to break through the bureaucracy that was not so much cruel as indifferent. This was the ultimate sin of the Bureau — the lack of response. For the most part, it could not even inspire the catharsis of honest anger. All was embraced by dullness, hopelessness, and boredom. What more could one do to a people?

Among the first white men to reach the American Indian were the missionaries — men doing well by doing good. On the northern plains, the tradition started with the noted Jesuit from Belgium, Father DeSmet, and it was carried on through many denominations and varying personalities up to the present time.

There were several reasons for the treatment and respect granted to Christian missionaries. For one thing, the Plains culture did not allow or provide for the luxury of extended torture. Even more important was the religious inclination possessed by the Indians. They had the greatest respect for the supernatural and for any ties to it. What the Sioux called "pejuta" has been mistranslated as "medicine." What it really meant was "a tie to supernatural powers and the ability to use those powers to further your own interests and ends." If the white missionaries showed sincerity and respect for their own God, who was the Indian to say him nay. On the other hand, as white military power grew and as the warriors lost battles, an inevitable thought arose. Since an Indian warrior received his strength and his prowess from his pejuta, then the man who beat him must have a stronger pejuta. The U.S. Army, then, indirectly set up the psychological basis for acceptance of the white man's religion. Religion meant power, and apparently the reverse was true — power meant religion.

This is not to suggest that all Indians immediately leaped into the arms of the Episcopalians, Congregationalists, and Roman Catholics assigned to the majority of the northern reservations. A few did immediately. They cut their hair, learned hymns, and tried to farm. More resisted, but they gradually edged toward a *pro forma* practice of the white man's religion. Still others reacted with total rejection — a rejection that in some families has remained up to the present time. It is safe to say that by the beginning of the twentieth century, most of the Northern Plains tribes were moving toward the Christianization of a majority, if not a totality, of their members.

Behind the whole business of Christianization was a body of governing policy and principle that extended back before the United States Constitution. Kipling called it "the White Man's Burden" in the nineteenth century; but it had earlier origins and roots that were deep and sometimes sincere. The terms "Christianization" and "civilization" were almost always used simultaneously and could not be entirely separated. The nineteenth-century mind in the United States and in most of the western world could not conceive of a true civilization based on anything other than Christianity. As a result, the United States, one of whose basic principles was the separation of church and state, forgot that founding maxim in an overwhelming desire to "lead the wretched heathens to the light" as Noel Coward once put it. The whole idea reached its culmination when U. S. Grant launched his Quaker policy in 1869. This provided that Indian agents should be chosen from the nominees of church bodies. All of this was done with the best and noblest of motives, but alas, it was found that those nominated by preachers were bigger crooks than the common, ordinary political hacks that the Indians were used to. Still, it depended on the individual man. A DeSmet, a Riggs, a Williamson, the German Jesuits who founded St. Francis Mission, and many others were men of probity, intelligence, and drive. The Indians respected them because they deserved respect. Such men won converts, and such men are remembered. Others feathered their own nests and provided a bad example of Christianity and civilization for everyone. They are forgotten, until bitter memories are brought to the surface, as they sometimes are.

It should be remembered that missionaries performed many functions other than the religious. They taught farming, dairying, homemaking, carpentry, and a myriad of other skills. Many Indians welcomed these. Others did not. Spotted Tail jerked his son out of the famed Carlisle Indian School because he thought that the youth was being trained to be a farmer instead of a chief.

Among the main things that the missionaries did was teach and translate. Most of the written forms of Plains Indian language originated in versions developed by missionaries who needed to translate the Bible into the formidably difficult tongues of the Plains Indians. This work was appreciated then and now. The men of the cloth also brought the first real teaching of the English language. This was urgent if the Indians were to deal with the new world that was overwhelming them. The methods were less than progressive. They taught English by trying to batter the knowledge of the Indian language out of the heads of small children. The word "batter" is used advisedly. Yet, as any good theologian from the Middle Ages would have told you, the end can justify the means for a believer; while many might disagree, the end was generally thought to be useful.

The missionaries possibly did more good than evil, but one would be hard put to prove it. There are still unanswered questions about the good fathers, pastors, brothers, and the like. If they were doing what they said they were doing and bringing a new life and a new hereafter to a grateful people, why did the old religion persist, and why did new forms of American Indian religion spring up? Consider as examples the Yuwipi ceremonies that started perhaps with Crazy Horse and continued up to the present time, the Ghost Dance religion which came from a Paiute in Nevada, and the Native American Church with its use of peyote which appeared in South Dakota on an organized basis shortly before World War I. It does appear that while Christianity appealed to many, and the older traditional forms to others, many were still grasping for something new and different. They rejected much of the old for losing its power, but were not ready to accept the white man's alternative. One of the alternatives led to the tragedy of Wounded Knee. Another, the Native American Church, embroiled them in legal controversy with the state and federal authorities for many decades. The third continues unabated.

All of this indicates that the Christian religion somehow failed. Possibly this was not because of its own flaws, but because it was attempting to bridge fundamental human gaps beyond the means of the people sent to practice and to preach.

Education was not the sole province of the missionary. The United States government, operating through the Bureau of Indian Affairs, had an interest both legal and chauvinistic in the processes. The Indian treaties required that the government establish schools for Indian students. In the Fort Laramie Treaty of 1868, the government pledged itself to provide one school and one teacher for every 30 students. This provision, which was to be periodically renewed and never completely dropped, was desired by both the government and most of the Plains Indian leadership. The government saw education as a prime means for "civilization." The more perceptive Indian leaders saw it as a device whereby the Indian youth could learn the white man's language and methods and perhaps beat him at his own game, thus insuring the survival of the people. Formal education took place originally in reservation day schools patterned after the one-room school house that was the basis of American elementary education. In time, the boarding school concept developed, and these institutions were placed both on and off the reservation. The final development was to place Indian students in the public schools of the various states. This advance did not come until the 1890s and has never been wholly implemented.

The Indians may have wished for educated children, but the process horrified them. Nineteenth-century education was certain of its values and its methods. If a student did not learn what he was supposed to or misbehaved, there was no recourse to guidance counselors or parental conferences — the teacher hit him. Many of the schools were run according to strict military discipline. The boys had their hair cut; they were put into stiff army shoes and woolen uniforms and were taught to march and drill. They received demerits for any offense against the rules of the school; this included speaking in their native language. This is undoubtedly a speedy and effective way to teach English, but it was a trifle hard on students who came to these institutions without knowing a single word of the English language. Severe trauma was frequently the result. Suicide rates rose and parents were disturbed. Many schools ran up against the pervasive influence of the grandmothers who consistently opposed white man's education. In the Plains Indian society, the grandmothers did most of the child rearing and were a strong force for traditional ways and against schoolhouses. Thus it became sort of a game. To educate an Indian, one had to catch him and catching him was frequently difficult. Students stayed away in such droves that the Bureau resorted to what can best be described as kidnapping to get them to school. Education under such unsavory conditions moved more slowly than usual and, as all of us know, education is a slow process at best.

As the educational system developed, it did not find its roots in the classical curriculum found today. Rather, it took its underlying philosophy from the experiments in educating the freed slaves conducted by the Freedman's Bureau and refined with considerable success by Booker T. Washington at Tuskegee Institute. This type of education was a combination of elementary reading, writing, and ciphering, combined with manual training, or in the case of girls, home economics. It is not by accident that Indian children and the children of freed slaves were mixed at Hampton Institute in Virginia in an early day. It is amazing how long it continued. The Rosebud boarding school did not graduate a high school class until 1939. Up to that point, the curriculum was still half academic and half manual training.

The Indians, of course, recognized what was happening. Some families decided it was worth it and pushed their children. Some outstanding successes resulted. Charles Eastman was a Santee Sioux who became a medical doctor and a famed writer. Chauncey Yellow Robe, a Rosebud Sioux who graduated from Carlisle, became a considerable leader of his people. Yet, there were more failures than successes, and those who were educated frequently met with rejection when they returned to their own people. The result was that while the literacy rose among the Sioux, the great mass of them received only the most rudimentary of educations. Many avoided it completely. The essential failure of the system was a result of the lack of acceptance of it by its clients. The mass of the Indian people were not convinced that it was **the** way. Instead they saw it as a means to break down their culture, language, and society. This was often too high a price to pay.

Perhaps the greatest failure of the white man, both as an agent of government and as a private individual, was his inability to provide a substitute for the great buffalo herds that were decimated from 1860 to 1880. The buffalo had provided the wherewithal for the existence of the Plains Indian people. They had provided the meat, the robes, the lodges, and the trade goods. Now they were gone. The result was something akin to the present-day United States of America if all industry and agriculture were wiped out in a 20-year period. The people were desperate, potentially starving, and clearly saw the end of their civilization. Such traumatic losses were brought about primarily by the penetration of the white man, with the aid of the Indians who hunted the buffalo in great numbers as an item of commerce. It was and is the single most important fact in Plains Indian history. It also is the greatest failure of the white man — and the Indians knew it.

The simplistic solutions of the Bureau of Indian Affairs stemmed from the fundamental beliefs of the American public that it served. The Bureau tried to turn the warrior into a farmer, to have him dismount from his war horse and then hitch him to a walking plow. Psychologically, it was an impossibility. Agriculturally, it was dubious in an area of insufficient rainfall. Economically, it never worked as it was intended. Some western Indians, such as the Corn Band of the Brulés, made an honest effort to become farmers, and some succeeded. By the turn of the century, a considerable cattle industry had grown at Pine Ridge, Rosebud, and the other western reservations. The "rich Indian" appeared. He did not last long. Bureau policies dictated the selling of the cattle herds in World War I, and they were never replaced. Breeding stock as well as the natural increase went at high prices, and the Indians were left with nothing as soon as the money was spent.

The failure to establish a viable economy, something that White America should have been able to do, meant the failure of all other policies. One need not be a Marxist to believe that stable society depends on people being able to eat regularly. Morale depends on people being able to support themselves. Education depends on the motivation that for one reason or another this education will serve a purpose. Because of the ultimate failure of the economy, everything else was unworkable. The great land grabs that came under the auspices of the Dawes Act of 1887 could never hav occurred if the Indians had had an economy that used the land productively. Thus it was that when the commission came to Pine Ridge in 1889 to get the signatures necessary to break up the Great Sioux Reservation, Red Cloud stated, "You have come to save us." The almost total dependency of the Indian on the United States Government for the most basic elements needed to sustain life meant that the tribes would lose in the negotiations over the land sales and cessions. The Indians had no high cards to play anymore. All that remained were sheer desperation and a feeling that all was slipping. Thus it was that responsible men sold and ceded vast amounts of tribally owned land. They had no choice. The alternative was starvation. No Indian leader with a sense of responsibility could accept that for his people.

How did the Indians view the white men who came? Some viewed them as saviours — on the cheap, of course. Others viewed them as rampaging land grabbers out to get anything they could. Anyone helping the Indians was appreciated and respected. Proud people were turned into beggars through no fault of their own. Here is the ultimate tragedy. The Indians of the period blamed the white man less then than we would today for destroying self-support and self-respect.

The white man penetrated the reservations, first as cattlemen and then as town builders during the first 15 years of the twentieth century. Most mingled closely with the Indians. Many took up the Indian land that had been released as surplus under the allotment system. The Indians finally saw the white man as a neighbor. While there were troubles, and mutual mistrust abounded, many strong relationships developed. This was the great period of the beginnings of intermarriage between the two peoples. Many of the formidable mixed-blood families trace themselves to liaisons begun from 1890 to 1914. A young Scotchman, "Scotty" Phillips, married Crazy Horse's sister. He became a famous rancher west of Fort Pierre and was highly instrumental in saving the buffalo. This he did because his wife's people believed that if the buffalo completely disappeared, they woo would disappear. Such actions and attitudes, while not universal, were common enough. In many cases, close friendships arose and continued through the generations down to the present time. In other cases, the mistrust continued. Familiarity does sometimes breed contempt. Yet, the Plains Indians for the first time saw the white man as he was — something other than a soldier, a government agent, or a negotiator after Indian land.

The common man finally came in contact with the Indians

on the Great Plains. Too much emphasis has been placed on the troubles between the two races when they were in contact, and too little emphasis is known of the good relations that developed between individuals. The white man became a husband, a lover, and a friend. These relationships were not on the level that has been much studied and has never been part of official policy. Yet, these are the fundamental relationships between the two peoples and on which better relationships can be built in the future.

The white man, through his government and his missionaries, never succeeded in completely imposing an alien civilization on an unwilling people. Yet, on a man-to-man relationship, the strengths of both can emerge and develop. It might be slow, it might take generations, and it certainly is not complete in 1974, but here lies the hope of the future. Individual dislikes, incidences of violence, and evidence of disrespect may be aspects of a passing phase.

Speaking as one who has lived most of his life in "Indian Country," it is my opinion that the Indian and the white man on the ranches and in the small towns get along much better than do the Indians as a people and the Whites as a people. The good sense and solid qualities of both groups must essentially provide the basis for a solution to the problems that each group causes the other. A view of the record makes it clear that these solutions will not come out of Washington, D.C., the Congress, or the courts. Above all, the historian, whose discipline concentrates on change functioning through time, must never lose sight of time. We must never forget that very little time has passed since Indian and white man came into close contact. Generations, not three-year crash programs, are necessary.

Selected Bibliography

American Indian Research Project, University of South Dakota. Oral History Collections.

Bourke, John G. *On the Border with Crook* (1891).

Cash, Joseph H. *The Sioux People* (1971).

Cash, Joseph H., and Gerald W. Wolff, *The Three Affiliated Tribes* (1974).

Cash, Joseph H. and Herbert Hoover. To Be An Indian (1971).

110

Collier, John. *The Indians of the Americas* (1947).

Deloria, Vine Jr. *Behind the Trail of Broken Treaties* (1974).

Duratschek, Sister M. Claudia. *Crusading Along Sioux Trails* (1947).

Eastman, Elaine Goodale. *Pratt: The Red Man's Moses* (1935).

Hyde, George E. *Red Cloud's Folk* (1937).

Hyde, George E. *A Sioux Chronicle* (1956).

Hyde, George E. *Spotted Tail's Folk* (1961).

Jackson, Helen Hunt. *A Century of Dishonor* (1881).

Kappler, Charles J. *Indian Treaties, 1778-1883* (1972).

Marquis, Thomas B. *Wooden Leg* (1931).

Marshall, S. L. A. *Crimsoned Prairie* (1972).

Meyer, Roy W. *History of the Santee Sioux* (1967).

Nabokov, Peter. *Two Leggins: The Making of A Crow Warrior* (1967).

Neihardt, John G. *Black Elk Speaks* (1932).

Utley, Robert. *The Last Days of the Sioux Nation* (1963).

Dale Crawford 76

The Quest For A Red-Faced White Man: Reservation Whites View Their Indian Wards

W. David Baird, University of Arkansas

The distinguished and talented corps of scholars who have preceded me carefully chronicled the different viewpoints that white and red communities had of each other during the first one-half of the nineteenth century. Professor Cash has just focused his attention on how the Indian viewed the white man during the latter part of that century. In order to complete the picture, it remains for me to consider the white man's views of the Reservation Indian during that same era.

To do so, frankly, is no easy task. The published and un-published material dealing with the subject is so extensive that it is virtually impossible to master. Moreover, there were as many viewpoints as there were observers. And not only did these views vary with individuals, but they differed with the particular Indian or Indians observed and with the time of the observation. As a consequence, any generalizations as to at-titudes held by particular groups are tentative at best. Yet, it is possible, I think, to detect certain mutually shared points of view among four classes of white observers — military, western, government officials, and reformers, including mis-sionaries. It is equally possible, given some margin for error, to illustrate the immediate and the long-range impacts of these views upon the red man. Much of this discussion, however, will not be new, especially to professional historians, nor can it be comprehensive. But hopefully it will be relevant to the purpose of this conference, following as it does the injunction of Dr. Samuel Johnson: "People need to be reminded more often than they need to be instructed."

For white Americans, the Gilded Age was a time of dramatic change. In less than 50 years, the economy of the nation altered from one emphasizing agriculture to one dominated by industry. Technological advancement was as real as it was apparent, providing Americans not only with the benefits of electricity but with such innovations as the phonograph, the telephone, and the twine binder, to name only three. Moreover, expanding opportunities for secondary, higher, and adult education brought the advantages of increasing literacy and trained professionals. With personal income increasing and the "good life" within the reach of most, Americans came to view their society as among God's most blessed. When fused with the Darwinian concept of "survival of the fittest" and the mission impulse of Christianity, this attitude rekindled a movement that had smoldered since the 1840s — "Manifest Destiny." Americans now came to measure other societies by the yardstick of their own, and when these were found lacking, they embarked upon a course of "enforced salvation." It was in this heady atmosphere of material success and philosophical justification that most white men formed their views of the reservation Indian.

Their attitudes were also affected by the immediate status of the red man. Presenting an impediment to western migration, the Plains Indians after the Civil War were assigned to specific reserves where the government hoped they could be induced to abandon their nomadic life and adopt settled agricultural habits. The objective was to provide instruction and subsistence during the transitional period, at the conclusion of which the Indian could join the predominant society, differing only in the color of skin. At best, the Plains Indian response to the government's policy was unenthusiastic; at worst, it resulted in wholesale rebellion and warfare. Whatever the reaction, it always led to the further involvement of white men and to the crystallization of their viewpoints.

This was particularly so in the case of the United States military. As might be expected, their views differed with particular Indians encountered and the circumstances of that encounter. Although few subscribed completely to the statement attributed to Philip Sheridan that "the only good Indian was a

114

dead Indian,"[1] most did agree with General Custer that when "stripped of the beautiful romance with which we have been so long willing to envelop him, . . . the Indian forfeits his claim to the appellation of the 'noble' red man."[2] This general conclusion that the Indians were no more than savages resulted from several observations and experiences.

For one thing, the appearance and personal habits of the red man offended the military. According to General Crook, the Indians were "filthy, odoriferous, treacherous, ungrateful, pitiless, cruel, and lazy." To be sure there was a positive side to their character, but it was "small" and "almost latent."[3] John Finerty, a war correspondent who adopted the military perspective, underscored this view, observing that most Indians were "greedy, greasy, gassy, lazy, and knavish."[4] Captain Eugene Ware was also convinced that instead of having noble features, "Indian men seemed to have a feminine look and the women to have a rather masculine look."[5] Like her husband and his colleagues, Mrs. George Custer was not impressed by the red man's appearance, either. She was most repulsed by the features of the older women — whom she called "hideous old frights" — who had thin and wiry hair, seared and lined faces, dull and sunken eyes, and huge orifices in the lobes of their ears. So repelled was Mrs. Custer that she applauded the Indian's use of paint, as "it certainly improve[d] the brown skin."[6]

If the military was disgusted by the appearance of the natives, it was even less appreciative of their cultural customs. Two Ninth Infantrymen in northern Wyoming in 1876 were so little impressed by a burial scaffold that they tore it down for firewood.[7] For Captain Ware and his comrades, the occasion of a council with Spotted Tail in 1864 provoked more mirth than solemnity. Upon receiving the peace pipe from the Indians, Lieutenant Williams wiped the stem under his arm and commented: "I don't believe I want to swap saliva with that crowd."[8] The accoutrements of the medicine man, however, more horrified than amused the army. A necklace of human fingers, a "bag filled with right hands of papooses" of enemy tribes, and different bags made of human scrota shocked even the seasoned command of Ranald Mackenzie.[9]

How the Indians conducted warfare — a cultural characteristic in the view of the army — was even more terrifying. The adjectives of "cruel," "inhuman," "barbaric" "treacherous," and "savage" punctuated most accounts. What evoked these descriptions were instances, real or fancied, of scalping, mutilation, and torture. General Custer reported how one captive trooper was "tied to a stake, strips of flesh cut from his body, arms, and legs, burning brands thrust into the bleeding wounds, the nose, lips, and arms cut off," and when senseless dispatched by knives wielded by youngsters.[10] Another account revealed that the body of a Negro scout was found with "about a dozen arrows shot in his breast and a picket pin [stuck] through his balls," while the body of a white trooper was located with a "smally piece of scalp taken and an arrow pushed up [its] anus."[11] Such reports convinced most soldiers that capture by the Indians meant sure torture, scalping, and death.

Although the troopers were outraged by the "uncivilized" warfare, they had grudging respect for the Indian as a warrior. Most agreed that he was an effective rifleman within 200 yards, although beyond that range, because of his inability to estimate distance and adjust rifle sights, he was inferior. General Nelson Miles attributed to him "courage, skill, sagacity, endurance, fortitude, and self-sacrifice of a high order."[12] Robert Carter thought "their fortitude, powers of endurance and wonderful powers of recuperation were almost marvelous."[13]

The ability to see an admirable side of the Indian's character was characteristic of many military men. Most discriminated between hostile and non-hostile bands, and practically all could express sympathy with the suppressed condition of their adversary. Indeed, some blamed the necessity for warfare upon inept agents, designing traders, and rapacious cowboys instead of upon the misdeeds of the Indians.[14] General Miles was absolutely enraptured by the oratorical skills of the Indians; and as "reason and logic held sway" in their councils, he thought them "the most democratic people in the world." "Whatever, may have been their history," said the General, "their blood and experience produced a superior race."[15] Accordingly, neither Miles nor most of his brother officers advocated a policy of extermination. General Pope once countermanded orders with that intent, labeling them "atrocious."[16] Sherman insisted that "we don't want to exterminate or even to fight them."[17] Even General Sheridan advocated only a policy of "punishment-shall-follow-crime."[18]

In many ways, the western viewpoint of the Indians was not unlike that of the army. They too condemned the red man for what they thought were uncivilized habits and

116

characteristics. As Howard Ruede wrote of the Omahas in 1877: "These men are a repulsive looking set: they have thick lips, big noses, and as their clothing is none too clean and what they have is just enough to cover their bodies, they don't present a very pleasing object to the eye. If the men are dirty, the women are filthy, for their work does not help to make them any cleaner."[19] "Dirty bodies, never washed except by the rains of heaven," also bothered another observer on the occasion of the Medicine Lodge negotiations in 1867.[20] And a Kansas editor expressed similar views of Kaw Indians who had just visited Topeka: "Those sweet-scented ones that were encamped near here have gone back to their reservation," he said. "When we consider how efficient they were in 'gobbling-up' the putrescent animal and vegetable matter about the city, we almost regret their departure."[21] Finally, the observations of Baylis John Fletcher, a cowboy who trailed cattle north from Texas to Wyoming in 1878, were typical. Admitting that his ideal of the Indian had been formed from reading James Fenimore Cooper, he recounted that he was speedily disillusioned when he met the real thing. "The human body in a state of savage neglect," he observed, "is the most repulsive object known to civilized mankind. The odor emitted by the bodies of those poor wretches was horrible, and their habits will not admit of description . . . . When at last they all departed, the sympathy I had felt for the poor outraged red man was gone."[22]

Like the army, the westerners also had little respect for the red man's culture. As Charles Goodnight put it: "Human though they were, their culture was that of a stone-age savage."[23] Uninformed as to "tepee etiquette," Mrs. Finan Roy of McPherson County, Kansas, was not amused when without warning an Indian once slapped her on the shoulder and yelled in her ear.[24] And the McCracken family of Jewell County, Kansas was not flattered when a group of Omahas came to their home and demanded something to eat. This event only confirmed their view that the Indian was little more than a beggar.[25] Such an opinion was also held by those who observed the refined art of Indian negotiations. On such occasions, the orations of the red man, their content, and the "grunts of approbations" received from listening tribesmen were considered as no more than the "whining[s] of humored beggar[s]" and the rantings of virtual idiots.[26] Frank A. Root was just as negatively impressed by a Kickapoo dance. He found the "discordant sound" of the drum "torturing" and "monotonous." To him, the costumes worn by the Indians were "outlandish and ludicrous," and he was astonished that no two tribesmen dressed exactly alike.[27]

Whites on the frontier also believed that the red man was guilty of theft, treachery, and cruelty. It was said that he would steal the tires from a man's wagon wheels while he was driving at a trot. According to one authority, "the settlers would take with them the cow, the coop of chickens, the stove, and practically everything they owned" when they would be absent from their homestead for an extended period.[28] That the Indian, moreover, was inhumane and cruel, in the view of the settlers, was an observable fact. In 1864, for example, Captain of Kansas Volunteers, H. E. Palmer, found that at one ranch hostile raiders had taken small children by the heels and beaten their heads into pulp by swinging them against the log house. The nude body of the hired girl was discovered staked out on the prairie full of arrows and terribly mangled.[29]

Given such experiences, according to many westerners, extermination of the red "vermin" was the only solution to the Indian problem.[30] This was particularly the view of frontier newspapers, who frequently urged the military to do its work *à la Chivington*.[31] Just as determined but somewhat more moderate was the view of the editor of the *Kearney Herald*. "Now and then," he wrote, "you will hear a chicken-hearted historian, who knows nothing of the red savage, extolling his noble characteristics and praising his natural knightly endowments. [But] the best and only way to reconcile the blood-washed animal will be to impose upon him a worse schooling than has ever befallen the inferior races."[32]

Although the belief that the Indian was a fierce and brutal red fiend underlay this cry for extermination, other western viewpoints reinforced it. For one thing, few frontiersmen believed that the red man was entitled to all of that land. In this they agreed with no less an authority than Theodore Roosevelt. "It cannot be too often insisted," he wrote in *The Winning of the West* in 1889, "that they did not own the land. . . . If the Indians really owned Kentucky in 1775, then in 1776 it was the property of Boone and his associates. To consider the dozen squalid savages who hunted at long intervals over a territory of a thousand square miles as owning it outright — necessarily implies a similar recognition of the claims of every white hunter, squatter, horse-thief, or wandering cattleman."[33]

Not only did the Indian not own the land, but in view of the westerner, he did not even use the land. "Why," one asked, should "a country one-third larger than the entire settled portion of the United States. . .be withheld from those who are now taxed to support the uncivilized hordes who now monopolize it for hunting grounds?"[34] Such a view continued even after the reservations were pared down, and it was prominent during the congressional debate over allotment. Senator Preston Plumb of Kansas declared that such a measure would place large tracts of land "under the blight of Indian occupancy." Moreover, it would create a "landed aristocracy" that would leave the treasures of the soil undeveloped.[35]

Yet, many westerners could and did appreciate the Indian's reluctance to part with his land or alter his occupation of it. Senator Henry Teller of Colorado declared "that you cannot make any Indian on this continent . . . , while he remains anything like an Indian in sentiment and feeling, take his lands in severalty. . . . It is a part of the Indian's religion not to divide his land." To do so was "a crime equal to the homicide of his own mother . . . and a violation of the moral law."[36] To Teller, allotment was a method "to despoil the Indians of their lands and to make them vagabonds on the face of the earth,"[37] and he prophesied that in time the Indians would curse the hand now raised professedly in their defense as having misunderstood "Indian character, and Indian laws, and Indian morals, and Indian religion. . . ."[38]

Those whom the Senator felt most misunderstood the red man were government officials and so-called friends of the Indians. Due to President Grant's Quaker policy, after 1868, many in the service of the Bureau of Indian Affairs were either active Christians or paid lip-service to Christianity. This plus the fact that most were non-western in nativity meant that their views would be of a different cast than those views predominant in the west. Though hardly a noble creature, the Indians to the westerners were an ignorant and helpless people who had a large moral claim against the government, a debt which could not "be discharged by gifts of blankets and bacon, or any routine official care for their protection or relief."[39] Instead, as we had taken "from them the possibility of living in their way," we were "bound in return to give them the possibility of living in our way. . . ."[40] Warfare, therefore, was to

119

be avoided, as it was better to feed the Indians than to fight them.[41] More importantly, many Indian officials believed that the red man had done nothing to deserve military retaliation,[42] as he was "tractable" and responded to "uniform kindness and justice."[43]

Although government officials tended to view the Indian with compassion, none would admit that he was civilized — a state that included the trinity of Christianity, individualism, and private property. They found all kinds of evidence to support this viewpoint. The superstitious beliefs of the red man, for example, were wholly antithetical to Christianity. The Sun Dance and its religious connotations was considered "barbarous and demoralizing. . ., antagonistic to civilization and progress."[44] Indeed, all dances were little more than "orgies," at which time men were "clothed more in paint and feathers than in civilized dress."[45] The lack of "citizen dress" also suggested the absence of Christian modesty.[46] Nor were the Christian virtues emulated by marriage without benefit of clergy or by polygamy.[47] "There are at the present time," concluded Commissioner of Indian Affairs E. A. Hayt, "no valid marriages among the Indians. . .," and he recommended that agents should be required to marry all men and women cohabiting together upon the reservations, giving them certificates of marriage.[48]

If the red man lacked Christian traits and habits, he was even more deficient in the attributes of individualism, a key element of civilization. The importance of this characteristic was suggested by Commissioner E. P. Smith: "A fundamental difference between barbarians and a civilized people is the difference between a herd and an individual. All barbarous customs tend to destroy individuality."[49] The lack of individualism was noted in several facets of the Indian's life, but especially in the governmental structure of the tribe. Honor and power went to the chiefs and warriors instead of to "intelligent, working, and progressive" individual Indians.[50] So esteemed tribal leaders had inordinate influence upon their people and thwarted their progress toward civilization.[51] Moreover, law and order was not a characteristic of reservations controlled by traditional leadership.[52] Commissioner Price noted that "women are brutally beaten and outraged; men are murdered in cold blood; the Indians who are friendly to schools and churches are intimidated and preyed upon by the evil-disposed; children are molested on their way to school, and schools are dispersed by bands of vagabonds. . . ."[53] Even when the guilty were apprehended, they failed to receive proper punishment. Price was particularly incensed that Crow Dog, the murderer of Spotted Tail, made recompense for his crime by giving Spotted Tail's family a number of horses. He was even more infuriated when the Supreme Court upheld the right of the Indians to adjudicate their own disputes.[54]

Not only did tribal government suggest the absence of individualism, but to federal officers it was also indicated by the refusal of the Indian to support himself by individual effort. As Quapaw Agent D. B. Dyer put it: "The majority are indolent. You can find them almost any day standing around their cabins or leaning around drowsily, like animals who have been hired to personate men and are tired of the job."[55] V. T. McGillycuddy of the Pine Ridge Agency saw additional evidence of the absence of individualism. Unappreciative of the red man's concept of sharing, he believed that the progressive Indian was denied the fruits of his labor because of the "Dennis Kearney" attitude — that is, the jealousy manifested by the less industrious toward the energetic tribesmen.[56] So long as that frame of mind and virtual communism prevailed, he believed, beneficial labor was impossible. Furthermore, the practice of issuing rations, according to some, did not encourage individual effort. "The result of help is helplessness," opined educator Alfred Riggs, adding for emphasis that continual dependence meant loss of independence.[57] Finally, Commissioner Smith believed that the "irregular habits of the wigwam" retarded personal initiative. The discipline essential to civilization could not be promoted by parents who had no idea of attire suitable for the classroom or spoke a language antithetical to progress.[58]

According to Smith, "the starting point of individualism for an Indian [was] the personal possession of his portion of the reservation,"[59] — or private property, the third manifestation in the trinity of civilization. That the Commissioner should link communal ownership of land with the absence of civilization was not unique. Indeed, it was a widely held view that there could be "no material advance in civilization unless landed property [was] held by groups at least as small as families."[60] Possession of property would inculcate pride and self-respect and give incentives for work where there had been none. And the work envisioned for the Indian was agricultural endeavor, a

121

certain sign of civilization. "Historians, philosophers, and statesmen freely admit," declared Commissioner J.D.C. Adkins in 1885, "that civilization as naturally follows the improved arts of agriculture as vegetation follows the genial sunshine and the shower."[61] Adkins and other officials were absolutely convinced that any society based upon hunting and communal ownership of property lacked the essential ingredients of progress and moral development.[62]

The viewpoints of the reformers — humanitarians, missionaries, and many eastern observers — of the Indian differed only in degree from those of government officials. On the whole, they were even more sympathetic to the red man. Senator Joseph Brown of Georgia declared, for instance, that the Indian was "not naturally disposed to go to war with the white man," and when he had, it was because he had "been provoked by white men or by the agents of the government."[63] Moreover, many believed that the native American was superior to the black man and would prosper if provided the same opportunities.[64] Wendall Phillips was convinced that the Indian was a creature of immense nobility. Their history was "a glorious record of a race that never melted out and never died away, but stood up manfully, man by man, foot by foot, and fought it out for the land God gave him, against the world, which seemed to be poured out over him." "I love the Indian," he emotionally announced, "because there is something in the soil and climate that made him."[65]

Despite pity, admiration, and love for the red man, few of his friends would admit that he fully measured up to the yardstick of civilization. Especially did he fall short in the realm of religion. The Sun Dance, considered a "religious orgy," was "too horrible for words," according to one observer.[66] Similarly impressed, missionary William Welch was just as shocked by the charms of the medicine men.[67] The Reverend William H. Ketcham, a noted Catholic missionary, proclaimed: "If you have ever witnessed the repulsive ceremonies that some Indians still practice, you will appreciate what you owe the Gospel."[68]

Men of the cloth and other reformers were alike appalled at what might be called the lack of Christian manners. The Indian men were "naked," except for a slight "cloth about the loins," causing William Nicholson to observe that they must have suffered a good deal from "wet feet."[69] Moreover, these wards of the nation gorged themselves without thought of the morrow, practiced polygamy, divorced easily, permitted unchastity, indulged in intemperance, raced horses, gambled and engaged in untruthfulness and improvidence.[70]

Like many government officials, the reformers also saw the lack of individualism on the reservation as indicative of the absence of civilization. The group orientation of the Indian and his deference to traditional chief and warrior leadership was believed to suppress this fundamental requirement.[71] Moreover, the nomadic habits of the Indians retarded the self-help efforts of individual members of the tribe.[72] Such efforts, according to some, were also impaired by the persistence of the native language. [73] Others, however, attributed the lack of individualism not to the cultural milieu of the Indian but to the government's failure to protect him before the white man's law. Because he lacked even the ordinary rights of American citizenship, he was unable to assert himself and to protect his property.[74]

Yet when it came to the appreciation of private property, practically all reformers agreed that the Indian was woefully deficient. Representative Thomas Skinner of North Carolina, for example, believed that the Indian was dependent, pauperized, mentally dwarfed, and lethargic because of the common ownership of lands on secluded reservations.[75] On the other hand, Senator Matthew C. Butler of South Carolina was not so sure that these difficulties stemmed from an inadequate understanding of property. How, he asked, could the Indians produce cereal unless they had some idea of land titles?[76] Yet even Butler agreed that agriculture was deficient on the reservation, a sure sign that if the concept of private property was understood, it was not properly practiced.[77]

Although the red man was lacking in civilization, no reformer believed that the Indian desired to perpetuate that state. Just as the Flatheads had once asked for the "book of heaven," the tribesmen of the late nineteenth century undoubtedly thirsted for Christianity and civilization.[78] Furthermore, the reformers did not doubt that the Indians could make the transition from barbarism. After all, the black man, "although broken down by long slavery," had "taken courage" and was "working very hard, often saving money to buy a farm and stock it."[79] Moreover, other Indians had adopted the white man's way, particularly the Cherokees, Choctaws, Chickasaws, Creeks, and Seminoles, and if they could, so could the reservation tribes.[80]

How to effect the passage from barbarism to civilization, however, often differed with one's point of view. General Custer believed it possible only when the Indian was pushed to such a physical extremity that he would have no other alternative. Some westerners thought it possible only if the Indian had the example of white farmers settled nearby. Captain Richard Pratt's motto was "Kill the Indian and save the Man" by means of education.[81] Missionary John C. Lowrie saw the solution in Christianity; "First Christianity, then civilization," he said.[82] Government agents tended to see it in terms of agriculture and private ownership of land, both considered to be essential to the basis of any moral development.

Given these varied viewpoints, it is possible to isolate specific policies and actions that emanated from them. The opinion of the military, for example, that the Indian was cruel and inhumane brought demands that the army assume responsibility for Indian affairs. Moreover, it frequently prompted equally cruel and inhumane responses. The famous encounters at Sand Creek, Washita, and Wounded Knee are familiar examples. Additionally, soldiers were frequently quick to fire even at friendly Indians.[83] And one military surgeon unnecessarily amputated a warrior's leg at the hip only to make a "damn good Indian of him."[84] Such responses seldom brought much remorse, especially among the rank and file. Following Wounded Knee, a Ninth Cavalry Trooper composed words of which the following is representative:

E battery of the 1st stood by and did their duty well,
For every time the Hotchkiss barked they say a hostile fell.

. . .

So all have done their share, you see, whether it was thick or
thin
And all helped break the ghost dance up and drive the hostiles
in.[85]

Yet not all in the military applauded such sentiment. General Miles, for one, believed Wounded Knee unjustifiable and injudicious.[86] Others, especially General Crook, thought so much of the military prowess of the Indians that they recruited them into their commands as scouts and guides. This view also led to the little-studied but novel experiment of enlisting regiments, troops, or companies of Indians as regular components of the army.[87]

The impact of western views is just as evident. Convinced of the treacherousness and cruelty of the Indian, the most dominant reaction following the Civil War was fear. Mrs. Sarah Finch of Custer County, Nebraska, for example, was so afraid of being ravaged by Indians that for three years she carried with her a box of sugar mixed with strychnine.[88] In the aftermath of the Indian wars of the 1870s, fear of the Indian turned into contempt and demands for dispossession. Believing that only white men could properly develop natural resources, westerners insisted first that the Indian be concentrated upon reservations and second that the reservation itself be abandoned. When Congress failed to act quickly enough to appease their demands, they physically occupied the red man's domain, establishing farms and laying out communities. They even protested, just as did Senator Plumb, the size of the tract eventually allotted the Indians and demanded that in the interest of progressive agriculture the white man be permitted to lease the allotment.

How the views of government officials and reformers shaped policy is equally apparent. Beliefs that the red man was heathen-like and immoral brought regulations that prohibited the Sun Dance and other dances, dismantled the structures where such ceremonies were conducted, required Christian marriages, barred the practice of giving away the possessions of deceased Indians, and forbade consumption of the blood and intestines of beef slaughtered for reservation distribution.[89] In complete sympathy with the regulations, the missionaries also sought to provide alternatives for those practices banned. In lieu of dances, they encouraged nothing less than baseball and croquet.[90]

In attempts to individualize the red man and to make him self-supporting, administrative efforts were made to redesign the tribal system of government and to restructure life styles and habits through education. In order to undermine the influence of the chiefs, agents created Indian Police forces and established Courts of Indian Offenses on the various reservations. Just as revolutionary were the efforts to inculcate individualism and self-help. Manual labor schools were established to educate young men in appropriate trades and agriculture arts and the young women in homemaking. English was decreed as the language of instruction, a regulation not altogether applauded by the missionaries. Convinced that the greatest Indian deficiency was the Gospel, they advocated the use of the native language as a means of teaching the Indian Christianity and of bringing him to fluency in English. Students in the government schools were also to receive training in patriotism and in history, the objective of which was to "create a spirit of love and brotherhood in the minds of the children toward white people. . . ." Officials also instructed that the students should be taught to appreciate Washington's Birthday, Arbor Day, and Franchise Day, the latter celebrating the passage of the Dawes Act.[91] So convinced was the Bureau of Indian Affairs as to the absolute necessity of this kind of education that they directed that parents should have their rations withheld if they refused to send their children to school.[92] Of the different types of educational opportunities available, however, government officials were unanimous in their view that boarding schools were the most compatible with civilization. Such institutions as Hampton, Carlisle, and Haskell took the child from the "irregular habits of the wigwam" and put him in the veritable bosom of the white man, facilitating the objective of a self-sufficient, patriotic, Christian Indian.

The final step in the civilization of the Indian was individual ownership of land. Convinced of the deficiency of the red man in this essential, government officials, reformers, and westerners joined in recommendations to Congress that eventually produced first the Indian Homestead Act in 1874 and then the Dawes Act in 1887. The latter measure directed the termination of tribal government and the allotment of the reserve to individual members of the tribe. Although some saw the act as a "last ditch" effort to preserve a vestige of the Indian's landed heritage, most hailed it as the culmination of the government's "vanishing policy," by which the red man would receive the private property from which the advantages of civilization flowed. Indeed, it would solve the so-called Indian problem and provide a compensation for the sins of the nation against its native population.

Clyde Dollar has suggested that, like Alice in Wonderland, red and white men should try to crawl through the looking glass in an attempt to understand their views of each other.[93] One wonders if the white men of the late nineteenth century would have profited from a similar exercise. Frankly, I doubt it. To them it would have been a fatuous experience. Imbued with the mission impulse of Christianity and convinced of the reality of the Darwinian concept of the survival of the fittest, they were wholly satisfied with the image reflected by the looking glass. To have crawled through would have meant compromise with heathenism—and compromise would have been sinful and indicative of weakness. As they saw it, then, there was absolutely no alternative to civilization; the Indian must become a red-faced white man.

Our age, however, is less positive in its definition of civilization, and perhaps our quest to see behind the mirror can be more successful. Although our Gilded Age counterparts could not, we can grasp the meaning of the scene described by E. C. Abbot, a cowpuncher on the Rosebud in 1883. The sun was just coming up when he saw an old Indian go up a hill to pray.

> He was away off on the hill [Abbot remembered later,] and he held up his arms, and oh, God, but did he talk to the Great Spirit about the wrongs the white man had done to his people. I never have heard such a voice. It must have carried a couple of miles. . . . It is a sight I will never forget. I am glad that I saw it. Because nobody will ever see it again.[94]

We will not see it, either; but like Abbot, we too must not forget it.

Notes

[1] See *Oxford Dictionary of Quotations*, 2nd ed., rev. (New York: Oxford University Press, 1955), p. 499.

[2] George A. Custer, *My Life on the Plains*, with an introduction by Edgar I. Stewart (Norman: University of Oklahoma Press, 1962), p. 13.

[3] Martin F. Schmitt, ed., *General George Crook: His Autobiography* (Norman: University of Oklahoma Press, 1960), p. 69.

[4] John F. Finerty, *War-Path and Bivouac* (Chicago: n.p., c. 1890), p. 107.

[5] Captain Eugene F. Ware, *The Indian War of 1864*, in *The Indian and The White Man*, ed. and with an introduction by Wilcomb E. Washburn (Garden City: Doubleday & Company, Inc., 1964), p. 284.

[6] Elizabeth B. Custer, *Following the Guidon*, with an introduction by Jane R. Stewart (Norman: University of Oklahoma Press, 1966), p. 87, 96.

[7] Don Rickey, *Forty Miles a Day on Beans and Hay* (Norman: University of Oklahoma Press, 1963), p. 233.

[8] Ware, *The Indian War of 1864*, in Washburn, ed., *The Indian and The White Man*, pp. 285-86.

[9] John G. Bourke, "The Medicine-men of the Apaches," *Ninth Annual Report of the Bureau of Ethnology, 1887-88* (Washington, D.C.,: Government Printing Office, 1892), pp. 481-82.

[10] Custer, My Life on the Plains, p. 162.

[11] Rickey, *Forty Miles a Day on Beans and Hay*, p. 232n.

[12] Nelson A. Miles, *Serving the Republic* (New York: Harper and Bro., Pub., c. 1911), p. 118.

[13] Robert G. Carter, *The Old Sergeant's Story* (New York: F. H. Hitchock, 1926), p. 85.

[14] Rickey, *Forty Miles a Day on Beans and Hay*, pp. 225-27; Richard N. Ellis, *General Pope and the United States Indian Policy* (Albuquerque: University of New Mexico Press, 1970), p. 41.

[15] Miles, *Serving the Republic*, p. 114.

[16] Ellis, *General Pope and United States Indian Policy*, p. 77.

[17] Carl Coke Rister, *Border Command: General Phil Sheridan in the West* (Norman: University of Oklahoma Press, 1944), p. 67.

[18] *Ibid.*, p. 147.

[19] Howard Ruede, *Sod House Days: Letters from a Kansas Homesteader, 1877-78*, ed. by John Ise (New York: Cooper Square Publishers, Inc., 1966), p. 17.

[20] Rister, *Border Command*, p. 54.

[21] Quoted in Marvin H. Garfield, "The Indian Question in Congress and in Kansas," *Kansas Historical Quarterly*, 2 (Feb. 1933), pp. 40-41.

[22] Baylis John Fletcher, Up the Trail in '79, ed. and with an introduction by Wayne Gard (Norman: University of Oklahoma Press, c. 1968), p. 38.

[23] Lewis Atherton, *The Cattle Kings* (Bloomington: Indiana University Press, 1961), p. 125.

[24] Everette Dick, *The Sod-House Frontier, 1840-90* (Lincoln: Johnsen Publishing Co., 1954), p. 165.

[25] Belle McCracken, "The McCracken Family of Jewell County, Kansas," *Kansas Historical Collection*, 17 (1926-28), pp. 413-14.

[26] "A Drive Through the Black Hills," *Atlantic Monthly*, reprinted in *Northwest Railroad* (Battle Creek: Wm. C. Gage & Sons), pp. 77-78.

[27] Frank A. Root, "Kickapoo-Pottawatomie Grand Indian Jubilee," *Kansas Historical Quarterly*, 5 (Feb. 1936), pp. 16, 17.

[28] Dick, *The Sod-House Frontier*, p. 166.

[29] *Ibid.*, p. 172.

[30] Lucile M. Kane, ed., *Military Life in Dakota: The Journal of Philippe Regis de Trobriand* (n.p., n.d.), pp. 17-18.

[31] Garfield, "The Indian Question in Congress and in Kansas," p. 43.

[32] Quoted in Robert W. Mardock, *The Reformers and the American Indian* (Columbia: University of Missouri Press, 1971), p. 86.

[33] Theodore Roosevelt, *The Winning of the West*, vol. 1, in Washburnn, ed., *The Indian and The White Man*, p. 132.

[34] Charles Collins, *Collins' History and Directory of the Black Hills* (Central City, Dakota Territory: n.p., 1878), pp. 7, 8.

[35] 46th Cong., 3rd Sess., Congressional Record (Jan. 26, 1881), p. 940.

[36] *Ibid.* (Jan. 20, 1881), pp. 780-81.

[37] *Ibid.* (Jan. 26, 1881), p. 934.

[38] *Ibid.* (Jan. 20, 1881), p. 783.

[39] *Report of the Commissioner of Indian Affairs, 1875*, p. 23.

[40] *Ibid.*

[41] *Report of the Commissioner of Indian Affairs, 1868*, p. 2.

[42] *Report of the Commissioner of Indian Affiars, 1874*, p. 272.

[43] *Report of the Commissioner of Indian Affairs, 1871*, p. 117.

[44] *Report of the Commissioner of Indian Affairs, 1884*, p. 37.

[45] *Report of the Commissioner of Indian Affairs, 1890*, p. 62.

[46] *Report of the Commissioner of Indian Affairs, 1873*, p. 8.

[47] *Report of the Commissioner of Indian Affairs, 1878*, p. 35.

[48] *Ibid.*, p. xxvii.

[49] *Report of the Commissioner of Indian Affairs, 1873*, p. 4.

[50] *Report of the Commissioner of Indian Affairs, 1874*, p. 5.

[51] *Report of the Commissioner of Indian Affairs, 1884*, p. 60.

[52] *Report of the Commissioner of Indian Affairs, 1873*, p. 4.

[53] *Report of the Commissioner of Indian Affairs, 1883*, p. xi.

[54] *Ibid.*, pp. xiii-xiv.

[55] *Report of the Commissioner of Indian Affairs, 1883*, p. 80.

[56] *Report of the Commissioner of Indian Affairs, 1884*, p. 39 and *1878*, p. 48.

[57] *Report of the Commissioner of Indian Affairs, 1871*, p. 444.

[58] *Report of the Commissioner of Indian Affairs, 1873*, p. 4.

[59] *Ibid.*

[60] Quoted in William T. Hagan, "Private Property, the Indian's Door to Civilization," *The American Indian: Past and Present*, eds. Roger L. Nichols and George R. Adams (Waltham, Mass.: Xerox College Publishing, c. 1971), p. 203.

[61] *Report of the Commissioner of Indian Affairs, 1885*, p. iii.

[62] *Report of the Commissioner of Indian Affairs, 1878*, p. 48.

[63] 46th Cong., 3rd sess., *Congressional Record* (Jan. 24, 1881), p. 881.

[64] 49th Cong., 2nd sess., *Congressional Record* (Dec. 15, 1886), p. 190.

[65] *Third Annual Report of the Board of Indian Commissioners, 1871*, p. 39.

[66] Phil Kovinick, "South Dakota's 'Other' Borglum," *South Dakota History*, 1 (Summer, 1971), p. 224.

[67] William Welsh, *Report of a Visit to Spotted Tail's Tribe of Brule Sioux Indians, Etc.* (Philadelphia: n.p., 1870), p. 14.

[68] *Report of the 26th Annual Meeting of the Lake Mohonk Conference, 1908*, p. 56.

[69] Welsh, *Report of a Visit*, p. 14; William Nicholson, "A Tour of Indian Agencies in Kansas and the Indian Territory in 1870," *Kansas Historical Quarterly* 3 (Aug. 1934), p. 295.

[70] Nicholson, "A Tour of Indian Agencies," pp. 296, 310.

[71] 48th Cong., 1st sess., *Congressional Record* (Mar. 26, 1884), p. 2280.

[72] Welsh, *Report of a Visit*, p. 10.

[73] *Report of the Commissioner of Indian Affairs, 1890*, p. CLI.

[74] 49th Cong., 1st sess., *Congressional Record* (Feb. 19, 1886), p. 1633.

[75] 49th Cong., 2nd sess., *Congressional Record* (Dec. 15, 1886), p. 190.

[76] 46th Cong., 3rd sess., *Congressional Record* (Jan. 20, 1881), p. 781.

[77] Welsh, *Report of a Visit*, p. 10.

[78] *Ibid.*, p. 14

[79] *Ibid.*, p. 9.

[80] *Report of the Commissioner of Indian Affairs, 1868*, pp. 17-18.

[81] See Hazel W. Hertzberg, *The Search for an American Indian Identity* (Syracuse: Syracuse University Press, 1971), p. 16.

[82] *Third Annual Report of the Board of Indian Commissioners, 1871*, p. 177.

[83] See John W. Hakola, ed., *Frontier Omnibus* (Missoula: Montana State University, 1962), pp. 281-82.

[84] Dan L. Thrapp, *Victorio and the Mimbres Apaches* (Norman: University of Oklahoma Press, 1974), p. xi.

85 Quoted in Stanley Vestal, *The Missouri* (New York: Farrar & Rinehart, Inc., 1945), pp. 240-42.

86 Miles, *Serving the Republic*, p. 243.

87 W. B. White, "The American Indian as a Soldier, 1890-1919" (unpublished paper delivered before the Northern Great Plains Conference of History, Sioux Falls, South Dakota, October 1973).

88 Dick, *Sod-House Frontier*, pp. 179-80.

89 *Report of the Commissioner of Indian Affairs, 1883*, p. xv, and *1890*, pp. CLXVI and 62.

90 Welsh, *Report of a Visit*, p. 19.

91 Estelle Reel, *Course of Study for the Indian Schools of the United States: Industrial and Literary* (Washington: Government Printing Office, 1901), pp. 143-44: *Report of the Commissioner of Indian Affairs, 1890*, pp. CLXVII-CLXIX.

92 *Report of the Commissioner of Indian Affairs, 1890*, p. XCLVII.

93 See Daniel Tyler, ed., *Western History in the Seventies* (Fort Collins, Colo. Educational Media and Information Systems, 1973), pp. 38-45.

94 E. C. Abbot and Helena Huntington Smith, *We Pointed Them North: Recollections of a Cowpuncher* (Norman: University of Oklahoma Press, 1955), p. 169.

Part Two

The Indian Response

The Indian Weltanschaung: A Summary of Views Expressed by Indians at the "Viewpoints in Indian History" Conference, August 1974, Colorado State University.

Daniel Tyler, Colorado State University

History

The formal criticism that has become an expected part of most history conferences usually focuses on the quality and content of prepared essays. The critiques range from a review of factual and bibliographical errors to the more general considerations that the authors might have presented. Those of us non-Indians who listened to the critique of the previous six papers were mildly surprised to hear a totally different form of criticism — one which says a great deal, in fact, about the Indian view of himself, his culture, and the historical process.

Dave Warren[1] set the tone by suggesting that in the Indian world view, the past is dominated by concern with the origin and destiny of the people. Having assisted a number of Indian tribes in the writing of their own history, Warren's conclusions are based on a considerable amount of field experience in addition to his own training as a historian. To him, the Indian world view of history approaches a metaphysical level in which statements and events are justified by means of myths, creation legends, and stories coming directly from the tribe. To explain the tribe's history, then, demands a unique set of terms and references which may not be familiar to non-Indian scholars. However, if the story of the Indian past is going to be comprehensible and relevant to present-day Indians, it has to be applicable to the pressures and problems of living today. In Warren's words, "If we are to learn anything from history, we are to learn how to apply [it] in our private lives, in our daily dealings with each other, Indian or otherwise." If the traditional stories serve to remind the people of the longevity and nobility of their culture, they need to be incorporated in the tribal history. At the same time, there may be an archaeological answer to historical questions that may seem to be at odds with traditional tribal interpretations. What is important, in Warren's view, is that the Indians from different cultures understand how they have functioned together and how they have managed to sustain themselves as a people with some kind of integrity as a given tribe from a previous time of origin.

In such a context, therefore, history will serve the Indians not only as a point of contact with their ancient heritage but as a viable force for strengthening tribal identity in the present. The search for "truth" is only one part of the historical process.

Along these same lines, Ruth Roessel[2] stresses the importance of Navajos writing their own history. The old people are the best source of tribal tradition. They know the stories which describe the origins of the people, their wanderings, and their trials and tribulations. In order to imbue the young people with the rich cultural heritage of the Navajo, says Roessel, the elders' stories must be used as a basis for writing texts and monographs for use in the schools.

We are dealing here with didactic history. It is intended to instruct the young so that they will be familiar with tribal traditions. It is aimed at counteracting the anti-Indian bias presented in existing histories. It is also a deliberate attempt to heighten the identity of a people who, since boarding school days, have been encouraged to abandon their "Indianness."

It is also clear that this kind of history is purposefully intended to be something unique and different from what the Indians have encountered in materials published by the dominant society. Since the older, more traditional style of history, written largely by non-Indians, has failed to help native Americans rectify the treaty violations, social problems, and suffering of the Indian people, readers are now seeing a new kind of history in which the writers will not be afraid to apply the lessons of the past to the present. Such an approach will most assuredly depart from the techniques of historical criticism laid down by Leopold von Ranke in the nineteenth century. But if history can be a force for social change, the Indians will gladly accept a modification of traditional methods.

Allen Slickpoo and Jim Jefferson note another dimension to the writing of Indian history.[3] Tribal histories need to be written by more than one person. They should be sanctioned by a committee of tribal elders or leaders, not so much because of the fear of exposing tribal secrets, but because the tribal stamp of approval serves the additional purpose of bringing the tribe together. History in this sense is a rallying point and a catalyst for tribal nationalism.

Within most tribal structures, a sense of unity and conformity have been dominant. One who stepped beyond the limits of his social, economic, or political position was quickly brought back into line through discipline or public ridicule. A greater emphasis on ethno-history would assist historians in understanding this characteristic and many others which combine to make the Indian cultures so distinctive.

Undoubtedly, Indian and non-Indian versions of the past will clash when the facts are compared. However, if it is better understood that history for the Indian people of today is serving a need which both reflects their second-class status in American society and their desire to preserve the myths and legends which were so functional one hundred years ago, the debate over factual accuracy will become academic. To hear an Indian insist that the Indians did not come to America by way of the Bering Strait generates a good argument among non-Indian anthropologists. If we pass through Dollar's "looking-glass" in an effort to understand how important it is for the Indians of today to establish their intellectual and traditional claim to the land, perhaps it is not necessary to dispute the point. To argue that the Indians were invaders like the whites contradicts their tribal lore and undermines their interest in establishing a singular identity. To do battle over the facts, it seems to me, is to deny that the Indian world view is different. History for them, at least at this time, serves a different cultural function. If non-Indians refuse to accept this fact, they have lost the fight against ethnocentrism.

Art and Education

Lloyd New's explanation of Indian art makes it possible to comprehend another aspect of the Indian world view.[4] Because of the tremendous change that has occurred in Indian culture in the past one hundred years, it has become increasingly important for Indians to search for a new sense of their native actuality. Since artistic expression is more personal than the writing of tribal history, there is no problem of tribal control; there are other problems.

As Chick Ramirez[5] makes very clear, few people agree on what Indian art really is. The non-Indian community has occasionally objected to art forms which do not follow the traditional, flat, one-dimensional style. Since art is more of a commercial pursuit than the writing of history, non-Indians have exercised a degree of control over Indian art forms in an attempt to conform the medium to the commercial market.

To insist, for commercial reasons, that Indians produce "traditional" art forms is to further emasculate their self-identity and the free expression of their emotions. Just as the writing of history reflects a cultural and national orientation to the most dominant forces in a society, so too the expression of an artist will follow certain trends as a society moves through different stages of development. As New points out, North American Indians never joined the melting pot. The experimentation in styles, media, and subject matter which is sometimes criticized for being non-Indian represents, in fact, the Indian expression of his search for belonging in a society which has rejected him. This determination to be different, to blend, if necessary, some of the traditional artistic tradition with the frustrations of modern society, is a logical expression of the Indian world view for the most recent historical period.

New also notes that the government now has to face the fact that 40 percent of the Indian population is non-functional. He blames this factor to some extent on the past educational practices in which Indians were trained to become farmers, technicians, and participants in white society. Their schools did not encourage the free expression of art as much as the learning of new skills which would lead to jobs in the Anglo-American culture of the United States. Assimilation has generally been the objective of government-sponsored Indian education, and the Indians of today, according to Shirley Hill Witt,[6] are persistently fearful that "the 'ultimate solution to the Indian problem' — the extinguishment of native Americans" will continue to threaten their culture.[7] Indians are also unhappy with the policy of give and take which has made federal money available during one administration and unavailable during another. According to Mary Pat Cuny Rambo,[8] Indians are just plain tired of being dependent on the government, not knowing from one minute to the next how much money they will have and how long it will last. Indians are also tired of the crash programs which are designed to resolve the educational problems in one fell swoop. For Rambo, the answer is community college education where Indians can function independently and in their own cultural milieu.

For the moment, then, Indians are determined to find their own unique way to express, describe, and experience their culture. Their desire for cultural autonomy is genuine; to malign their techniques or channel their interests is to continue the mistakes of the past. How the Indians arrived at this point and what can be done to make their own transitional progress smoother and more meaningful are subjects which scholars might consider when they decide to study the twentieth century.

[1] Director of Research and Cultural Studies of the Development Section, Institute of American Indian Arts, Santa Fe, N.M.

[2] Director of Indian Studies, Navajo Community College, Chinle, Arizona.

[3] Allen Slickpoo is Director of the Nez Perce History and Culture Project; James Jefferson is a Tribal Writer for the Southern Ute Project.

[4] Director of the Institute of American Indian Arts, Santa Fe, N.M.

[5] Denver-based Indian artist.

[6] Professor of Anthropology, Colorado College, Colorado Springs, Colo.

[7] Shirley Hill Witt, "Native Women Today," *Civil Rights Digest*, v. 6, no. 3 (Spring, 1974), pp. 31, 35.

[8] Community College, Macy, Nebraska.

Indian Humor: Can The Red Man Laugh?

R. David Edmunds, University of Wyoming

The answer to the question embodied in the title of this paper is, "Yes; obviously, Indians can laugh." In fact, a close examination of early travel literature and other white accounts of Indian society records instance after instance of Indian humor. Anyone familiar with modern Native Americans knows them to be a fun-loving people, continually joking, often in the face of adversity.[1]

Yet the Indian stereotype, nurtured in white literature for more than three centuries, pictures just the opposite. As early as the seventeenth century, white writers portrayed Indians as products of the primeval forest, "hellish fiends and brutish men." Cotton Mather referred to Indian leaders as "horrid sorcerers, and hellish Conjurers, and such as conversed with Daemons." These images more resemble characters from a Gothic Romance, than a people imbued with a natural sense of humor. Indeed, Mather's description could as well picture the witches of Shakespeare's *Macbeth*, as the Indians of Massachusetts.[2]

Such characterizations continued through the eighteenth and nineteenth centuries and into our own time. In eighteenth-century Kentucky, the depiction of Indians as subhuman brutes was best epitomized by a white frontiersman's assertion: "I've tried all kinds of game, boys! I've fit bear and painter and catamount ... but There ain't no game like Ingins — No Sir! No game like Ingins."[3]

Francis Parkman, writing in 1851, described the typical Algonquian warrior of the old Northwest as a man with a hard and stern physiognomy. Ambition, revenge, envy, jealousy are his ruling passions; . . . . [He is] overcast by much that is dark, cold, and sinister . . . . In his feasts and his drinking bouts we find none of that robust and full-toned mirth which reigned at the rude carousals of our barbaric ancestry. He is never jovial. . . . Over all emotions he throws the veil of iron self-control . . . a mask of icy coldness.

and John Greenleaf Whittier, in the "Bride of Pennacook," states:

The Indian's heart is hard and cold
It closes darkly o'er its care
And formed in nature's sternest mold
Is slow to feel and strong to bear.[4]

Yet, throughout the nineteenth century, at the same time that Indians were being described as hard-hearted stoics, the image of the noble savage also was emerging. This image painted the Indian in more complimentary colors, but it still portrayed him as a mirthless individual, rarely smiling and possessing little sense of humor. Cooper's Chingachgook and Uncas may be noble, but they certainly aren't fun-loving pranksters.[5] Indeed, as Vine Deloria, Jr., has pointed out, "the image of the granite faced grunting redskin has been perpetuated by American mythology."[6]

However, as I suggested at the start of this paper, other, more careful observers described Indians as jovial people, much given to practical jokes and clowning. Ethnologists such as George Bird Grinnell and Clark Wissler attempted to dispel the old stereotypes.[7] More recent writers, such as Deloria and Nancy Lurie, also point out that modern Native Americans have a keen sense of humor. They suggest that white Americans might better understand the Indian community if they investigated what made Indians laugh. It is such an investigation that I hope to pursue.[8]

First of all, a brief discussion of joking relationships is needed, since such systems institutionalize humor within the fabric of human society. As anyone vaguely familiar with traditional Indian society knows, many tribes established formal joking relationships between members of the same kin group in order to maintain a stable system of social behavior. Such relationships varied from tribe to tribe, and were used for several purposes. Teasing was utilized to enforce tribal mores and to point out personal deviances to individuals. Other joking relationships, especially between certain family members of opposite sexes served as a formal means of ameliorating uncertain situations which could prove hazardous to the family structure. A good-natured joking relationship therefore provided a Fox warrior with a ready-made behavior pattern for approaching his sister-in-law. There was no uncertainty involved. He could banter her in a friendly manner, and he expected her to reciprocate in kind. Of course, this railery could involve a wide variety of subjects, but the important point is that such humor was an integral part of everyday life. It seems unrealistic therefore, that whites would picture Indian society as stoic, cold, and devoid of laughter.[9]

Let's turn then, to the situations that provoked such laughter among the tribes of North America. Psychologists argue that whatever the subject matter, most humor is based upon such elementary human reactions as surprise, incongruity, or feelings of superiority. Much traditional Indian humor incorporated these qualities.[10]

The element of surprise was utilized best by Indians through the use of practical jokes, and many observers agree that Indians *were* notorious practical jokers.[11] John Stands in Timber recounts that as a boy among the Cheyennes, he and some of his companions took great delight in harassing the Horse Men, a religious society among the Cheyenne warriors. According to Stands in Timber, the boys waited until the society was meeting inside a teepee, holding their religious rites. The boys then supplied the society with its namesake. They opened the flap and pushed in a half-wild yearling colt. Needless to say, as the frightened yearling sped about within the confines of the teepee, the religious ceremonies were terminated. Stands in Timber also remembers that sometimes practical joking almost went too far, as when another Cheyenne, Little Hawk, hid all the arrows in camp just prior to a horse raid by an enemy war party.[12]

Perhaps the classic example of Indian practical joking emerges from the pages of Frank Linderman's *Plenty Coups: Chief of The Crows*. According to Plenty Coups, a Crow warrior named Medicine Raven would go to any lengths to gain a laugh at the expense of his companions. During the third quarter of the nineteenth century, a Sioux war party attacked a white outpost in Montana. The raid took place in the dead of winter, but a band of Crow warriors, including Medicine Raven, pursued the raiders, overtook them near the Black Hills, and in the ensuing skirmish killed several of the Sioux warriors. The Crows then returned to Montana, bone-tired and suffering from hunger and cold. Upon their arrival back at the outpost, several whites rushed out to greet them and to thank them for their assistance. Medicine Raven and most of the other Crow warriors were wrapped in heavy buffalo robes, but as the white traders approached, Medicine stuck a hand through the folds of the robe to receive the traders' handshakes. A trader named Paul McCormack was the first to encounter Medicine Raven, and he reached down, seized the hand, and gave it a hearty shake. He immediately jumped back in horror. Medicine Raven had cut a hand off one of the fallen Sioux and had thrust the severed limb through his robe. When the white man grabbed it, Medicine Raven had let go and the frozen hand was pulled completely out in the open. Medicine Raven convulsed in laughter. McCormack turned pale.[13]

Incongruity also played an important role in red humor. Anything that seemed strange or out of place could be the source of much amusement. Wissler describes the uproar of laughter in a Blackfoot camp when one end of a role of trade calico was attached to a horse's tail and the animal sent racing through the village, unrolling the bolt and eventually dragging fifty yards of material behind him. In fact, the Blackfeet thought the incident so funny, that other Indians hurried to imitate it, and within a few minutes, more than one hundred horses were dashing madly about, trailing similar bolts of newly received annuity calico.[14]

Native Americans also were much amused by deformities among the whites they encountered. In the seventeenth century, Father Biard, a Jesuit serving among the Indians of Canada asserted that:

> You do not encounter a big-bellied, hunchbacked, or deformed person among them. . . . . Any of our people who have some defect, such as the one-eyed, squint-eyed, and flat-nosed, are immediately noticed by them and greatly derided, especially behind our backs, and when they are by themselves. For they are droll fellows, and have a word and a nickname very readily at command if they think they have any occasion to look down on us.[15]

A similar situation, only in reverse, arose on the southern

plains during the nineteenth century. In this incident, some Kiowa warriors encountered a party of whites in western Oklahoma. One of the white men was wearing a pair of spectacles from which one of the lenses was missing. A Kiowa noticed the one-lensed spectacles, grinned, and asked to see them. Upon receiving the glasses, he abruptly turned and bolted back to his party. He soon returned, however, accompanied by another warrior. As they approached, the whites broke into laughter. The Kiowa had placed the one-lensed spectacles on a one-eyed friend.[16]

In his volume, *Custer Died for Your Sins*, Deloria points out that much Indian humor is at white expense. Indeed, Deloria's essay on Indian humor is filled with quips, puns, and other jokes directed at white men. Indian humor often has followed such a pattern, and psychologists argue that humor of this type may have a dual role. It may indicate feelings of superiority, or it can serve as a defense mechanism against oppression. If humor is used against oppression, it often is a powerful weapon, and may, in itself, become an agent for social change.[17]

Indian humor emerging from the first contacts between red and white men probably reflects a feeling of Indian superiority. Since Native Americans at first encountered Europeans in small groups, there was little reason for them to fear the pale-skinned strangers, and, after watching the ill-planned attempts of the Jamestown settlers to survive the Virginia winter, Indian people within Powhatan's confederacy would be justified in feeling themselves superior to such bunglers.

Yet much Indian humor of this sort was obtained at the expense of the French. Many of the early French explorers evidently possessed a healthy respect for the strange animals found in the New World. Pierre Liette, a French official in the Illinois Country, describes how he was enticed into a Peoria village and offered a seat of honor before the leading shaman of the Peoria tribe. Liette seated himself upon a pile of skins that had been spread upon the floor of the shaman's wigwam. The Indian busily was packaging herbs, powders, and other tools of his trade and readily answered the Frenchman's questions regarding Indian medicine. After a few minutes, Liette noticed that all of the other Indians in the wigwam had withdrawn to a far corner and were watching him with broad smiles on their faces. He then realized that the very skins on which he was seated seemed to be squirming beneath his legs. Startled, he asked the shaman what was under the skins. Unabashed, the old medicine man told him not to worry. It was only a few rattlesnakes from which he recently had extracted the venom.[18]

East of the Illinois country, in upstate New York, the Jesuits bore the brunt of Iroquois joking, since the sturdy fathers continually mispronounced the Iroquois language. Yet the Jesuits among the Iroquois fared better than their black-robed brothers to the north. Father Biard, among the Montagnais along the St. Lawrence Valley, registered a stronger complaint. Father Biard and his Jesuit companions hired some Montagnais to teach them the Algonquian dialects so that they might preach to the surrounding tribes. The Montagnais accompanied the Jesuits on their rounds and the Jesuits would give the Montagnais sentences in French which the Indians would translate orally back to the priests in Algonquian. The priests then would speak the Indian sentence to the audience. All seemed well, except that the priests were puzzled by a tittering that occasionally swept through the assembled Indians. Finally, the Jesuits realized the cause of the suppressed laughter. Their Montagnais translaters, in the words of Father Biard, had "palmed off on us indecent words which we went along innocently preaching for beautiful sentences from the Gospels."[19]

In more recent times, Indian humor has become more bitter, as the tribes saw their lands overrun by whites. It is from this situation that some of the sharpest Indian humor has emerged.

In 1870, while touring the East, Red Dog, a heavy-set old Sioux warrior, was asked to speak to a crowd of whites in New York City. Among the crowd was a former soldier who had known the warrior as a young man, and who chided him about his obesity. Unperturbed, Red Dog replied, that yes, as a young man he had been slim, but that he had always had an appetite for liars, and since so many white men now had moved west, he had been stuffing himself for several years.[20]

White duplicity was the subject of another Indian anecdote. During the 1850s, a small military expedition was sent onto the southern plains to meet with a band of Comanches and to convince them to make peace with the United States. Accompanying the expedition as guide and interpreter was Black Beaver, a Delaware famous for his service as a government

146

scout. The whites met with the Comanches and the commanding officer attempted to convince them of the power and numbers of white Americans. Since Black Beaver had been to Washington, the officer instructed him to tell the Comanches about the white man's steamboats. Black Beaver had seen steamboats and he spoke at some length. When he finished, a murmur arose from the assembled Comanches. "What did they say?", asked the officer. "They said they don't believe that damned lie," was Black Beaver's reply. The officer then instructed the Delaware to tell the Comanches about railroads. Black Beaver complied, and the same murmur emerged from the Comanches. "What did they say?" again asked the officer. "They don't believe that damed lie," came the reply. Perplexed, the white man then ordered the interpreter to tell the Comanches about the telegraph. Black Beaver was unfamiliar with this new invention, so he asked the officer to describe it. After the description was completed, the Delaware remained silent. "Why don't you tell them?" asked the officer. "Because," replied Black Beaver with a gleam in his eye, "I don't believe that damned lie myself."[21]

Such sarcasm was carried into the reservation period. John Stands in Timber drolly recounted that when he initially was around large numbers of whites at the Indian Agency, he at first assumed that the phrase, "Hey, you son-of-a-bitch" was the white term for "hello." Indians on another reservation were fascinated by a parrot kept by one of the traders. Since the parrot was given to reciting large strings of profanity, they named the bird after the agency blacksmith. Perhaps the champion of reservation sarcasm was Spotted Tail, chief of the Brulé Dakota. Spotted Tail had been visiting the agency headquarters where he had attended a formal dinner given in his honor by the commanding officer. At the dinner, many officers and their wives were assembled, but the post doctor kept chiding the Brulé chief about his traditional customs and manners, including his practice of maintaining several wives. Finally, Spotted Tail grew tired of the banter and replied, "Doctor, you come to my camp, I give you plenty to eat, good bed, and a wife to sleep with. I have been in your camp three days, and you no offer wife to me once." The doctor and his wife soon left the party.[22]

Perhaps the best collection of modern anti-white jokes can be found within Deloria's first volume, but he missed a few which are worthy of our attention. One of the most clever is a recipe for Dog Head Stew, by Dorothy Pennington. According to Pennington, the recipe is as follows:

> Carefully prepare one medium dog head, removing teeth from jaw bones, and hair, putting these aside for future use. Into kettle, add heaping handfuls of Camas bulbs and cattail roots. The eggs from two medium size salmon may be combined with water to cover, and place over fire and bring to a boil for three hours.

> It is customary to observe the rites of preparation in order to have all present appreciate the dish that will begin the feast.

> At the proper moment, using the ceremonial arrow, impale the dog heead and bring forth for all to observe the excellence of the dish.

> Then allow fifteen to thirty minutes for all whites to excuse themselves and leave for home. Bury stew in back yard and bring forth the roasted turkey with all the trimmings. In this way, a 15 pound turkey will do nicely.[23]

Government bureaucracy also has been the butt of many red jokes, but one of the best was a cartoon featured in the January 1974 edition of *Wassaja*:[24]

Implementing Our Indian Programs

As proposed by the
Interagency Task
Force

As specified by the
Bureau of Indian
Affairs

As designed by the
Army Corps of
Engineers

As produced by the
International Foundation
To Help Those Poor
Indians

As installed by the
Department of Housing
and Urban Development

What we really
wanted

Custer jokes continue to be legion among modern Native Americans, but most of them are of a recent origin. The Northern Cheyenne, however, have a traditional "Custer story." This anecdote pokes both fun and humiliation at the "boy general," but it originated prior to the twentieth century. The Cheyenne story opens in November 1868, with Custer's attack upon Black Kettle's village, along the Washita River in western Oklahoma. The Cheyenne say that an old Indian woman, hiding her two grandchildren in a ravine, was forced to watch as Custer killed her daughter and another grandchild. She survived the massacre and afterwards fled north to the Cheyenne bands in Montana, but her hatred of the white officer was not forgotten. She was present in the Indian village on the Little Big Horn, on June 25, 1876, when Custer and his command were overrun by Sioux and Cheyenne warriors. The Cheyenne story asserts that Custer was not killed in the initial battle, but was left alive and mortally wounded on the battlefield. Here, the old woman found the white officer, unconscious, lying on his back, face up among the sagebrush. Realizing that Custer soon would die, and not wanting him to enter the spirit world through an honorable, soldier's death, the old woman screamed for one of her friends, an immense Cheyenne woman, known as the Fat One. The Fat One, suffering from a glandular disorder, was so large that she could not ride a horse. Eventually, however, she came panting up the hillside. After listening to the old woman's pleas, the Fat One waddled over to the officer, lifted up her skirts, and plunked her bare backside down squarely on his face. Poor Custer — smothered into eternity.[25]

Of course, the story is apocryphal, but as one of my Arapaho students at Wyoming pointed out, can you imagine its impact upon dyed-in-the-wool Custer buffs?

Finally, there is an important strain within Indian humor in which Native Americans continue to laugh at themselves. Given the problems that Indians have faced through the past three centuries, such laughter is not only admirable, it's remarkable. The roots of such humor go back to the traditional tribal societies. Contradicting the stereotype of icy stoicism, there are many accounts of Indian mimicry and clowning. Father Le Jeune described the seventeenth-century Montagnais acting like buffoons, contintually poking fun at their chiefs and headmen, and cavorting about their camp like "wild ass colts." During the 1840s, Lieutenant James Henry Carleton witnessed Pawnee dances in Nebraska in which Pawnee boys would steal into the dance circle and mimic the adult dancers through exaggerated pantomime behind their backs. According to Carleton, the adult dancers accepted such antics good-naturedly, and the boys elicited much laughter from the Pawnees assembled to watch the ceremonies. Clowning and mimicry also was seen among the Comanches. In *Indians of the Plains*, Robert Lowie argues that such clownish behavior was a common trait of all the Plains tribes, and that upon certain festive occasions, warriors would dress themselves in outlandish costumes, get astride the worst nag they could find, and cavort about in a ridiculous or even obscene fashion.[26]

Some of this self-depreciation, like the joking relationships, was institutionalized and served as a form of social control. Studies of the Trickster, a mythological figure whose comic antics were part of the oral tradition of many tribes, indicate that the figure caused Indians to laugh at themselves, but also was used to teach tribal values and mores. Among some tribes, including the Zunis, certain ceremonial clowning provided an outlet for tension.[27]

Indian jokes upon themselves also involve problems they encountered mastering the white man's language. John Stands in Timber mentions two incidents of this nature among the Cheyenne. One incident involved a mixup over tobacco. Since "store tobacco" was in short supply on the Cheyenne reservation, the Cheyenne people tried to stretch it as far as possible. After smoking a pipeful of tobacco purchased at the trading post, they would save the ashes, scraping them out of the pipe, and then mix the residue with kinnikinick, or Indian tobacco. The warriors who were familiar with this process called the residue "powder." One Cheyenne warrior, however, after tasting the mixture for the first time in a friend's lodge, found the mixture pleasing and asked his friend what he had mixed with the kinnikinick. "Powder," came the reply. "Powder?" repeated the first Indian. "Yes," asserted his friend, "It's from the trading post." Unfortunately the novice smoker's only experience with "powder" had been with gunpowder. Yet, knowing his friend to be an honest man, he tried mixing and smoking some of his own. The results were as you might imagine. Although he was not hurt seriously, he received a broken pipe and singed eyelashes.[28]

Another mistranslation took place in Oklahoma after the

150

turn of the century. In this incident, some boys who had returned home from boarding school were trying to teach their friends in the village to play baseball. This story is quite involved, but it ends with a beginning baseball player being told to run for home and slide in if he wanted his side to win the game. He did — but he upset the soup kettle inside his parents' teepee.[29]

In conclusion, I have one more story, which again illustrates that Indians can laugh, and best of all, indicates how well the Sioux people of South Dakota have kept their sense of humor through recent periods of conflict and adversity. During the spring I spoke at Northern State College, at Aberdeen, South Dakota, and this story was told to me by a Sisseton Dakota. Like many other Indian stories, this one is a little bawdy, but I think you'll enjoy it. According to my friend, at the start of World War I, two young Sioux men from the Cheyenne River Reservation decided to enlist in the navy. Since they never had been off the reservation, they planned to take the train to San Francisco and to enlist after they arrived. The train ride across the Rockies was interesting, but it didn't fascinate them half as much as the hustle and bustle of the San Francisco waterfront. They left the train and walked around for several hours when they began to get hungry. They saw no restaurants, but one of them finally spied a man with a vending cart over which a sign announcing "Hot Dogs" was hung. Now, as my friend in Aberdeen tells it, since they were Sioux, they thought they were familiar with such a menu, and so they decided to give the man's product a try. They walked over to the vender and ordered two servings. He took their money and handed them each a sandwich wrapped in a small paper sack. As they walked away, one of the young men opened his sack, stared at the bun, took it out, looked inside, turned pale, and then in disbelief, turned to his friend and asked, "My gosh! What part of the dog did he give you?"

Notes

[1] I am indebted to Professor Lynne Dunn, of the Department of English, University of Wyoming, for his assistance in compiling materials for this paper.

[2] Michael Wigglesworth, "Devil's Den," in Henry Nash Smith, *Virgin*

Land: The American West as Symbol and Myth (New York: Vintage Books, 1950), p. 4; Roderick Nash, *Wilderness and the American Mind* (New Haven: Yale University Press, 1967), p. 36-37. Also see Leslie A. Fielder, *The Return of the Vanishing American* (New York: Stein and Day, 1968). Fielder devotes an entire volume to the image of American Indians.

[3] Arthur K. Moore, *The Frontier Mind: A Cultural Analysis of the Kentucky Frontiersman* (Lexington: University of Kentucky Press, 1957), p. 95.

[4] Francis Parkman, *The Conspiracy of Pontiac* (New York: Collier Books, 1962), pp. 61-62; John Greenleaf Whittier, "The Bride of Pennacook," *The Complete Poetical Works of John Greenleaf Whittier* (Boston: Houghton, Mifflin and Co., 1894), pp. 23-33.

[5] Roy Harvey Pearce, *The Savages of America: A Study of the Indian and the Idea of Civilization* (Baltimore: Tohns Hopkins Press, 1965), pp. 200-212.

[6] Vine Deloria, Jr., *Custer Died for Your Sins: An Indian Manifesto* (New York: Avon Books, 1970), p. 148. Hereafter this volume will be cited as *Custer Died for Your Sins.*

[7] George Bird Grinnell, *Blackfoot Lodge Tales* (Lincoln: University of Nebraska Press, 1962), p. 224; Clark Wissler, *Red Man Reservations* (New York: Collier Books, 1971), pp. 46, 77, 232, 280-281. This volume originally was published as *Indian Cavalcade* by Sheridan House in 1946.

[8] Deloria, *Custer Died For Your Sins,* p. 148; Nancy O. Lurie, "An American Indian Renascence?" in *The American Indian Today,* eds. Stuart Levine and Nancy O. Lurie (Baltimore: Penguin Books, 1968), p. 317.

[9] Harold E. Driver, *Indians of North America* (Chicago: University of Chicago Press, 1972), pp. 382-384; William H. Martineau, "Model of the Social Functions of Humor," in *The Psychology of Humor,* edited by Jeffrey H. Goldstein and Paul E. McGhee (New York: Academic Press, 1972), pp. 103, 111. Hereafter this article will be cited as Martineau, "Model of the Social Functions of Humor," and the volume will be cited as Goldstein and McGhee, *Psychology of Humor.* Also see Fred Eggan, ed., *Social Anthropology of North American Tribes* (Chicago: University of Chicago Press, 1972). This volume discusses joking relationships among many tribes.

[10] Patricia Keith-Spiegel, "Early Conceptions of Humor: Varieties and Issues," in Goldstein and McGhee, *Psychology of Humor,* pp. 4-34.

[11] Richard Irving Dodge, *The Plains of the Great West* (New York: Archer House, 1959), p. 308. Also see Reuben Gold Thwaites, ed., *The Jesuit Relations and Allied Documents,* 73 vols., (Cleveland: Burrows Bros., (1896-1901), 1:272. Hereafter these volumes will be cited as *Jesuit Relations.*

[12] John Stands in Timber and Margot Liberty, *Cheyenne Memories* (New Haven: Yale University Press, 1967), pp. 103-104, fn. 15.

[13] Frank Linderman, *Plenty Coups: Chief of the Crows* (Lincoln: University of Nebraska Press, 1962), pp. 264-265.

[14] Wissler, *Red Man Reservations*, p. 46.

[15] Thwaites, *Jesuit Relations*, 3:75.

[16] Mildred P. Mayhall, *The Kiowas* (Norman: University of Oklahoma Press, 1962), p. 58.

[17] Deloria, *Custer Died For Your Sins*, pp. 148-149; Martineau, "A Model of Social Functions of Humor," p. 104-112. Also see John H. Burma, "Humor as a Technique in Race Conflict," *American Sociological Review* ii (December 1946): 710-715.

[18] Milo Milton Quaife, ed., *The Western Country in the 17th Century: The Memoirs of Antoine LaMothe Cadillac and Pierre Liette* (New York: Citadel Press, 1962), pp. 149-150.

[19] Thwaites, *Jesuit Relations*, 51:137; 3:197.

[20] Katherine C. Turner, *Red Men Calling on the Great White Father* (Norman: University of Oklahoma Press, 1951), p. 125.

[21] Dodge, *The Plains of the Great West*, pp. 309-310.

[22] Stands in Timber and Liberty, *Cheyenne Memories*, p. 290; Wissler, *Red Man Reservations*, p. 77. Also see Shirley Hill Witt and Stan Steiner, eds., *The Way: An Anthology of American Indian Literature* (New York: Vintage Books, 1972), p. 75.

[23] Dorothy Pennington, "Dog Head Stew (for Fifty People)," in Witt and Steiner, *The Way*, pp. 75-76.

[24] *Wassaja*, May 1974, p. 9.

[26] Thwaites, *Jesuit Relations*, 6:243; Lieutenant James Henry Carleton, *The Prairie Logbooks: Dragoon Campaigns to the Pawnee Villages in 1844, and to the Rocky Mountains in 1845* (Chicago: The Caxton Club, 1943), p. 103. Also see Eugene Elliot White, *Experiences of a Special Indian Agent* (Norman: University of Oklahoma Press, 1965), pp. 307-309; Robert H. Lowie, *Indians of the Plains* (New York: McGraw-Hill, 1954), p. 129.

[27] Paul Radin, *The Trickster: A Study in American Indian Mythology* (New York: Schocken Books, 1972), p. 207; Jacob Levine, "Regression in Primitive Clowning," in Jacob Levine, ed., *Motivation in Humor* (New York: Atherton Press, 1969), pp. 167-178. Also see Frank C. Miller, "Humor in a Chippewa Tribal Council," *Ethnology: An International Journal of Cultural and Social Anthropology, vi* (July 1967): 263-271.

[28] Stands in Timber and Liberty, *Cheyenne Memories*, p. 280.

[29] *Ibid.*, pp. 280-281.

Dale Crawford 76

The Twentieth Century

Vine Deloria, Jr., Golden, Colorado

In recent years, there has been an increased interest in
Indian history, as much by Indians as by non-Indians, and the
result of this renewed interest is now bubbling to the surface in
Indian affairs. A lot of Indians are now asking historians,
"When in the hell are you people going to reach the twentieth
century?" The question seems to me to be a valid question,
because even a superficial survey of written materials on Indians shows that historians have concentrated on the Indian
wars of the Great Plains almost to the exclusion of other topics.
The usual format is to begin the book at the Minnesota war in
1862 and to carry the wars to their conclusion at Wounded
Knee in 1890, reciting all of the skirmishes that occurred in
between with particular emphasis on Red Cloud's war and the
desperate flight of Chief Joseph. Absent these figures, the run
of the mill historian would be unable to write about Indians at
all.

The ignorance of historians has to be a studied ignorance,
a teeth-gnashing determination to concentrate on familiar
topics to the exclusion of reality, if necessary; if any general
statement can be made about writing Indian history, however,
it is that almost every book comes to a screeching halt in the
December snows of Wounded Knee, and the fortunes of the
tribe from 1890 to the present are almost as obscure as the
prehistory of the tribe. Thus many Indians are not pleased that
historians can tell us precisely what Lewis and Clark had for
breakfast on the Bitterroot in 1804 but are unable to even guess
what happened to Indians following the Indian Citizenship Act
of 1924, or to name the current chairman of the tribe they
profess immense expertise and knowledge about.

In large measure, historians are responsible for the image which the American public has concerning Indians, because they are so fascinated with Chief Joseph, Crazy Horse, Geronimo, and Roman Nose that they spend all their energy reciting the exploits of these famous warriors and lead the public to believe that the real Indians are those who wear feathers, conduct endless hostilities, and poetically reject the overtures of the white man. In refusing to move beyond Wounded Knee to cover the very important things that have happened to Indians in the immediate past, people are led to believe that the worst events of Indian history happened during the Indian wars and that the best leadership was expended during those wars, leaving a miserable group of survivors who have somehow managed to eke out an existence until the present time.

It is difficult to understand why historians would choose to concentrate their efforts on this particular period, 1860-1890, because if you examine many of those battles very carefully, you will note that we won most of them. Stanley Vestal, in his book, *New Sources of Indian History*, compared the results of twelve battles between the Sioux and the cavalry and discovered that the Sioux had very good results when fighting the army. They killed more than five times as many soldiers as they lost and they wounded four times as many as they had wounded. Most of the Indian wars did not end with an Indian surrender but with the United States determined to bring peace at almost any price. The army campaigned against the Plains tribes during the summer of 1866, spent $30 million, lost hundreds of soldiers, teamsters, and scouts, and finally had to take a back seat to the Peace Commission, which made the 1868 treaties, because the United States would have gone bankrupt trying to defeat the Plains tribes.

At best, the record of the white man's valor in fighting the Indians is bad. This record does not come out in present historical analyses of the Indian wars, however, but the '60s and '70s are made to appear like John Wayne movie scripts, with drama oozing out of each page. This drama is reflected in the manner in which people learn to visualize Indians even today. When those people from Wounded Knee went on the Cavett Show, they had to wear wigs, to pretend that they didn't speak English and needed an interpreter, and perform other demeaning but easily identifiable acts in order for the American public, and some members of the ABC staff, to relate to them.

The best and most popular of the Indian war books is, of course, *Bury My Heart at Wounded Knee* by Dee Brown. The book is tremendously exciting and incorporates a lot of good material which had not been placed in its human context before, and perhaps this is the genius which undoubtedly shines through the book into the reader's sense of humanity. Dee Brown himself is a delightful gentleman with a great personal sense of balance. He did not hit the college lecture circuit even during the height of the book's popularity, because he did not want to be placed in the position where he would be considered a voice of the Indian. He appeared as an expert witness in the trial of Russell Means and Dennis Banks in Minneapolis, giving excellent and important testimony on the meaning of history.

It therefore seems likely that no one can accuse Dee Brown of having shirked his task as a writer or of having exploited Indians without returning something important to the Indian community. Yet the impact of the book on the public was another thing. It was so powerful that it focused the concern which otherwise might have been expended on living Indians on the atrocities of the past. The average housewife reading the book was ready to rush out into the backyard and serve cookies and cocoa to Dull Knife's Cheyennes should they come by on their flight to Montana. At the same time, her husband and neighbors were absolutely eager to strip mine Indian reservations, take Indian water for their swimming pools, push Indian fishermen off the rivers, and allow all kinds of violent and vicious abuse to be visited on the Indians of today. No one could see the connection between the Indians they were reading about and the Indians who lived down the road a piece.

If it were simply that Whites were getting the wrong information, whereas Indians knew their history intimately and accurately, the problem would be manageable — but such is not the case. A great many Indians depend on history books for their own knowledge of Indian history as it relates to other events in America's past and a number of dreadful mistakes have already been made by Indians who knew little or nothing about the past. Some years back when Glenn Emmons was Indian Commissioner, he had a favorite solution for the "Indian problem." He wanted to take the federal budget for Indians, divide it among the enrolled federal Indians, and reduce it by degrees by allowing no more Indians to receive funds after the last enrolled Indian had died. The plan was considered so ridiculous when it was suggested that Bureau of Indian Affairs personnel held their breath when asked by Emmons if the plan was worthy of consideration.

The plan died long ago, disgraced and without implementation, and nearly everyone who had known of the plan had forgotten it when a young Indian activist suddenly proposed the Emmons solution one day on national television. He had not been around when the plan was first suggested and had not even known that it was once a favorite plan for the anti-Indian element in the executive branch. He figured that it was a reasonable option to suggest for getting the Bureau of Indian Affairs off the full bloods' backs, but the plan was really not original, even with Emmons. It had been proposed during the 1920s when minerals of considerable value were being found on Indian lands. The plan at that point was to purchase all Indian lands and pay off the whole Indian population by a lifetime annuity from the federal government.

The point that must be made is that there is so little good information available on the problems of Indians in the twentieth century that an absolutely bizarre plan such as this can be put forward almost every 20 years as a totally new suggestion on how to resolve the continuing problem of providing federal services for Indians, without anyone recognizing that the plan has already been rejected several times in this century. If one considers some of the startling revelations of recent years, that Indians are bilingual, that they should control their own schools, that the tribal governments should be given more powers, it is apparent that this generation has done little more than repeat the suggestions of former generations which appear to be new and innovative because their cyclic emergence has not been recorded in any good history of Indians in the twentieth century.

Once we get both Indians and historians beyond the charge at Beecher's Island and into the twentieth century, we will discover that a great many things which people believe today are simply not true. The Bureau of Indian Affairs, for example, did not always have the rigid control it now exercises over every phase of Indian existence. The statute books are full of references to tribal self-government of a more profound nature than any we find today. The Quapaws, for example, had their own legislature and passed acts which governed them.

When they wanted a change in their relationship with the United States, they passed an act and had Congress endorse it. The Senecas made leases which were incorporated into federal laws passed by Congress and the tribe used this means of pinning down legal responsibilities for land use.

Almost the whole of today's generation of Indians rants and raves against the General Allotment Act of 1887 as the act of Congress which allowed the reservations to be broken up into small allotments. Yet few Indians know that the act itself did not allot the reservations. It gave the President authority to seek agreements from the respective tribes which would allow the government to purchase surplus lands from the tribe and allot the reservations to the individual tribal members. The Bureau of Indian Affairs, of course, pushed this policy relentlessly, making some tribes accept allotment who were obviously not ready to deal with individual ownership of lands. But the important aspect of allotment is the individual agreements made by the tribes with the different commissions that were sent to negotiate land cessions from them.

In many instances, the tribes made much better deals than one would have expected. The Umatillas, for example, negotiated an agreement which made the road through their reservation a toll road and rates for the passage of horses, sheep, and cattle were listed in the agreement. Even the Great Sioux Agreement of 1889, while its legality is dubious because of the numerous techniques used by the commission to get the necessary three-quarters approval of the adult males as required by the treaty of 1868, was not wholly without its redeeming features. It brought forward all articles of the 1868 treaty which did not deal with lands and annuities and may have preserved certain jurisdictional features of self-government which can be used by the Sioux tribes today.

The second aspect of the allotment process that is not widely known is that the basic act was amended in 1891 to allow the sick, elderly, and minors to lease their lands. It was not long before the bureaucrats had figured out how to classify almost every Indian in the tribe under one of these categories, and it was this law that made it possible for the Bureau of Indian Affairs to control large tracts of Indian land even against the wishes of the Indians. When the original landowners died and the allotments fell into heirship status, another law was passed in 1902 permitting Indians to sell their heirship property, and so the process was established whereby the government could both lease and sell individual allotments through subverting the philosophy and intent of the Dawes Act. Rather than protesting the Dawes Act, both Indians and historians should concentrate their research and energies in an examination of the succeeding acts to determine their validity and the background information which would be necessary to force the government to acknowledge its failure to carry out the spirit of these acts.

During the Wounded Knee crisis, we heard much talk about tearing up the Oglala Sioux Tribal Constitution and going back to the traditional way of life. It sounds like a good idea, but when we probe back into the history of the Pine Ridge reservation, we discover that the task would be very complex. Prior to the First World War, the Oglala Sioux had started the allotment process, but they had leased only one 40-acre tract to a non-Indian. During the war, their cattle were sold under the guise of helping the war effort. After the war, white cattlemen moved in force onto the lands of the reservation under new government leases, and the people have not yet been able to oust the process of leasing their lands to the Whites. Some of the tribal income today derives from this lease of Indian lands, and so eliminating the tribal constitution would involve such fundamental change that the tribe might be thrown into decades of poverty while it straightened out its finances.

Yet there is even another side to this problem. When John Collier held his Indian congresses during the spring of 1934 in an effort to get the Indians to approve the Indian Reorganization Act as he had written it, many of the full bloods actively opposed the I.R.A., arguing that those Indians who had sold their lands had in reality left the tribe and should have no votes if the new law were to be considered in a tribal referendum. Some of the Sioux full bloods were very vocal about keeping the allotment process intact and turning down plans for tribal land consolidation. When the elections were held to approve the I.R.A., the Bureau insisted that those who didn't vote "no" had in fact voted "yes" by their absence and thus it took an affirmative vote against the law to exempt a tribe from its operations. When one considers that the traditional Indian manner of voting "no" is to refuse to vote, the treachery of the Indian Bureau in forcing this law on the Sioux is apparent. But what can be done now? Perhaps the first thing is to clarify the history of the respective reservations as they entered the New Deal era to determine exactly how they looked upon that whole program which Collier put into effect.

It is this dark and treacherous area of the more recent past that frightens both Indians and historians because it makes Watergate look like quite a moral affair. Some government officials were hardly upstanding characters. Most of the members of the Dawes Commission authorized to allot the Five Civilized Tribes had hidden interests in oil companies and townsite development companies which were directly benefitting from the manner in which the lands were allocated among the classes of Indians eligible for lands. James McLaughlin, the U.S. Indian Inspector who pushed through so many allotment agreements, had more dirty tricks than Gordon Liddy and his plumbers; it is all there in the record, if one wishes to look at it.

It should be a number one priority of Indians today to get historians working on the policies, programs, and events of this century because unless we have a much better knowledge of what has gone before, we will continue to make dreadful mistakes based upon our inadequate knowledge of what has happened before our time. About two years ago, the Mancari case was decided by the Supreme Court, and Indian preference was declared to be constitutional. It was not long before the National Tribal Chairmen's Association passed a resolution asking that Congress abolish Indian preference because their "friends" in the Bureau knew them better than did other Indians.

The resolution was, of course, part of the hand-in-hand cooperation that N.T.C.A. and the Bureau of Indian Affairs have enjoyed since 1971 and was designed to block any meaningful progress in getting Indians in control of the Bureau. At least part of the motivation of the people supporting that resolution was their ignorance of their own history. Treaties, agreements, and statutes have many references to Indian preference, not simply in employment, but in appointments to office, in establishing land values and determining boundaries and land cession territories. Indian preference was a dearly bargained right a century ago, because there were very lucrative annuity freighting contracts to be gained. Even in the field of education, Indian chiefs of former years bargained for Indian preference so that their educated young people could have jobs when they returned from the government schools.

Rather than defending Indian rights, N.T.C.A. was in effect asking Congress to override a dearly purchased treaty right, and no one knew enough about Indian political history to raise even a question about what they were doing.

The profound ignorance which we see today concerning Indian history in the recent past sometimes takes on ludicrous overtones. A recent development of the National Congress of American Indians has been the Henry M. Teller Award which is given to that member of Congress who does the most for Indians each year. Whoever established the award had little knowledge of who Henry Teller really was because while Teller was a stalward defender of Indians when the allotment act was proposed, he was also a stalwart defender of the men who defrauded the Kickapoo Indians of Oklahoma. Angie Debo, in her book, *A Short History of the Indians of the United States*, recounts how Teller was suspected of taking bribes to cover up the scandal.

But perhaps the N.C.A.I. had good reason for giving the award, because their 1974 winner was Senator Gaylord Nelson, who some years earlier had taken most of the best lands of the Red Cliff Chippewas. The 1975 winner was Senator Henry Jackson, who for years had pushed termination in the Pacific Northwest. The N.C.A.I.'s Teller Award may be one of the double or triple ironies of history.

The failure to understand events of the immediate past also leads to an inability of people in the present to understand the events that engulf them. The Indian wars did not really end at Wounded Knee. The Chippewas at Leech Lake had an incident in 1898, the Paiutes and Navajos were still fighting sporadically as late as 1915, and the Lumbee Indians spooked the Ku Klux Klan in the 1950s. There has always been a potential for armed resistance in Indian country as long as there has been injustice perpetrated on Indians by the federal government. The fact of Indians taking up arms several years ago at Wounded Knee, therefore, can be seen in a much longer historical perspective as one of a continuing series of incidents where Indians have reached the point of utter frustration and have decided to force the government to act.

There have also been instances where Indians have very skillfully used the political institutions to gain their ends. In 1912, the Supreme Court handed down the *Sandoval* decision which gave a definitive answer to the question of whether the

Pueblos of New Mexico were protected by the full range of federal trust responsibilities. The result of that decision was to place in question the titles of lands within the old Pueblo grants which had passed out of Indian hands since New Mexico had become American territory. A tremendous struggle ensued following the decision, which was not resolved until the Pueblo Lands Act of 1924 which established the Pueblo Lands Board to determine which lands were being held illegally by non-Indians. A special attorney was appointed to represent the Pueblos, and in the next dozen years, nearly 3,000 white squatters were evicted from the Pueblo lands.

The solution finally reached in the Pueblo lands controversy could easily be used in determining the land titles and the interpretation of the series of Sioux treaties, agreements, and alleged agreements which made up the very complex legal history of the confiscation of the Black Hills territory. It is very much within the realm of possibility that Congress could set up a special commission to determine the legality of the taking of the Black Hills and the form of land restoration and financial compensation which is now due the Sioux Nation because of the illegalities of the past. But unless a significant number of people know the Pueblo history and the impressive precedents set in settling that problem, they cannot advocate or understand how to come to grips with the Black Hills problem, which partially triggered the Wounded Knee protest.

One of the most important things that both Indians and historians can do right now is to look into the controversies of this century and record from those people still living their recollections of incidents of a half century ago. Rather than attempting to rebuild the memories of the Pueblos regarding Coronado and the revolt of 1688, people should right now be doing extensive writing and interviews of the elder Pueblo people concerning how they organized and eventually won the battle for their lands in 1924. A Pueblo who was in his early twenties in 1924 would be in his early seventies now and would have sufficient memories to be a credible witness to the reality of history as he experienced it. The same would be true of other tribes and other important incidents of this century. Even the people who were young during the first days of the Indian Reorganization Act are now in their fifties and sixties and would have valuable information that should be preserved.

Instead of things getting better, they are getting worse. In

1958, the Colville Tribe of Washington got some surplus lands restored to it under the condition that the tribal council would develop a plan to terminate the tribe and present that plan to Congress within five years. Many of the leaders fought very hard against the implementation of that plan, but eventually those in favor of termination got into control of the tribal government and made an urgent push for implementation of terminal legislation. When a number of us were working at Colville in 1970 to prevent terminal legislation from being approved by the tribe, we discovered that most of the people did not understand how the issue of termination ever rose at Colville in the first place. People who are unable to remember the past are incapable of understanding the real alternatives that face them in the present.

Perhaps the most important part of Indian history is the available documentation that can be used to determine exactly what happened and what is meant. When we consider the plentitude of materials available on the twentieth century, it seems absurd to have to advocate that scholars concentrate their efforts on this period. The materials are absolutely overwhelming. Agency reports cover almost everything one can imagine, from family trees to the school supplies used in the day schools, from tribal land leases to minutes of forgotten council meetings where a variety of decisions were made which still affect Indians today.

In the broader perspective, one can determine that termination did not spontaneously arise on the Klamath reservation in 1954 and mysterious and ruthlessly overwhelm the Klamath people. They began as early as 1926 to try to break the hold of the Bureau of Indian Affairs over their forest, because they saw the deadly coalition of big timber companies and Bureau employees that were consuming their forest and returning them few benefits either in employment or in income. As more and more records on Klamath are read, the story emerges of how they attempted to use the Indian Reorganization Act to get rid of the Bureau and how that collapsed; and finally the meeting in Klamath Falls in 1947 where the people, so totally frustrated all their lives, began to demand any solution that was quick and relatively painless, just to be able to spend a few years in peace before they died, having been involved in this struggle for freedom from the Bureau of Indian Affairs *all their lives*!

Other stories are equally spectacular. In 1928, the Senate Indian Committee authorized an investigation of Indian conditions in the United States; every year until 1936, different Senators held field hearings around the country asking the Indians on the different reservations what should be done to simplify Indian affairs. Many Indians attended these hearings and presented their ideas and those ideas were not radically different from the ideas given to Robert Bennett when he was Commissioner of Indian Affairs and toured the country in 1966 asking for ideas. In fact, some of the same people attended both series of meetings. The point is not so much that very little was done, but that the continuing focus of concern during the century was the solution of perennial problems without a historical context within which those problems could be understood as something fundamental and important.

A good illustration of this principle is the continuing conflict between Indians and conservationists. One would assume that if ever two groups had a common ground it would be Indians and conservationists, but such is not the case. The first conservation movement resulted in the loss of millions of acres of Indian lands which were set aside by executive order as national parks and forests. The guiding philosophy behind this confiscation of lands was the preservation of selected areas for posterity, but the manner in which Whites wished to preserve the lands did not at all coincide with the manner in which Indians wished to preserve them. The Indians saw reverent use for ceremonial purposes as a high value in the conservation of lands, but the Whites saw the natural features as having a uniqueness that had to be captured by tourists on two-week vacations. Almost the same attitudes prevail today when Indians and conservationists clash, and neither side seems capable or willing to find a common understanding regarding nature.

Bob Thomas, the noted Cherokee wit and philosopher, once noted that Indian Affairs is comparable to a grade "B" movie. You can go to sleep and miss a long sequence of the action but every time you look at the screen it's the same group of guys chasing the other group of guys around the same rock, and no matter when you enter or leave, the plot and characters seem to be the same. It is this "sameness" that we have to overcome and only by becoming willing to charge into the freshness of the twentieth century will we be able to overcome the past and understand the present.

It is imperative that Indian history move immediately into this century, whether or not historians consider the twentieth century to be history. We are fast approaching the final decades of this century, and we have been without any discernible Indian policy since 1958, when termination was practically abandoned by the Interior Department. Since that time, both Congress and the executive branch have operated on an ad-hoc, let's-put-out-the-fire, basis which has served neither the federal government nor the Indians but has only postponed the solution of longstanding problems. When one gets a good perspective on the twentieth century, then the nature of these problems is illuminated so that the problems which plague Indians are seen as indications of a long process of change of cultural and economic forms which repeat basic patterns over and over again.

We search, in many ways, for the grandeur and nobility which shines out from the life stories of Crazy Horse, Chief Joseph, and other great leaders, but we fail to recognize that the same nobility can be reincorporated in Indian life today. We have but to bring historical consciousness of the whole Indian story to full light in order to regain the values which we cherish and admire from the heroic past. We can do no less for this generation and for the generations coming after us than to give them a sense of reality which can only come to people with a history.

Index